He Said,
She Said

This Side For Men Only
(Joking About Women)

———— • ————

by

Jack Kreismer

RED-LETTER PRESS, INC.
Saddle River, New Jersey

ACKNOWLEDGMENTS

EDITORIAL:
Jeff Kreismer

•

BOOK DESIGN & TYPOGRAPHY:
Jeff Kreismer

•

COVER ART:
Andrew Towl

•

CONTRIBUTORS:
Pat Pereira
Alix Perrault
David Reyneke
Kobus Reyneke
Mike Ryan
Jennifer Tomlinson

Red-Letter Press, Inc.
P.O. Box 393
Saddle River, NJ 07458

www.Red-LetterPress.com

He Said,
She Said

She Said: You get me so frustrated and so annoyed that I can't think straight.

He Said: I didn't mean to push all your buttons. I was just looking for mute.

A doctor examines a woman, then goes into the waiting room and says to the husband, "I don't want to scare you, but I don't like the way your wife looks."
The husband says, "Me neither, but she's a wonderful cook and is good with the kids."

Harvey gets pulled over for speeding. "I'm gonna help you out," says the cop. "Give me a good excuse and I won't write you a ticket."
"Three weeks ago, my wife left me for a cop," Harvey explains. "So when I saw your car coming, I thought you were trying to bring her back."

"Marry an orphan: You'll never have to spend boring holidays with the in-laws." -*George Carlin*

She Said: Can't you ever pay me a compliment?

He Said: Sure. Mosquitoes are attracted to you.

"Women wear a pair of panties but only one bra."
-*Gallagher*

She Said: You should start exercising to lose that gut.

He Said: Yeah, maybe I'll start with the exercises you do- didley squats.

Satan walked into Duffy's Corner Tap Room and planted his pitchfork firmly on the floor for maximum effect. He cast his evil gaze over the customers, who jumped up and ran out in fear. In seconds, the once-crowded bar was empty save for one old man. The Devil strode up to the old-timer and hissed, "Don't you know who I am?"
"Yeah, I know who you are," the old man replied, never looking up from his beer.
"Well, aren't you afraid of me?"
"Afraid of you?" the old man said with disdain. "Why should I be afraid of you? I've been married to your sister for 32 years."

She Said: Honey, what actually is reincarnation?

He Said: It's when you die and come back as something totally different.

She Said: So I could come back as a pig?

He Said: You're not listening to me, are you?

"Sometimes if a woman has a really nice butt she'll wear tight pants. And then everyone looks at her butt when she walks by. That's nice, but it seems like a waste. Everybody's looking there, I feel like we should put important information on the butt. We should put the photos of missing children right on there." *-Demetri Martin*

He Said: So am I being treated to your favorite dessert tonight?

She Said: We'll see. What's your favorite dessert of mine?

He Said: Sara Lee Apple Pie.

"What are the three words guaranteed to humiliate men everywhere? 'Hold my purse.'"
-*Francois Morency*

"It can take a man several marriages to understand the importance of monogamy." -*Jason Love*

A woman is standing before the judge in a packed courtroom. The judge asks, "What is it that you stole from the grocery store, ma'am?"
"Only a small can of a half dozen peaches," pleaded the woman.
"That'll be six nights in jail- one night for each stolen peach," declares the judge.
The woman is crestfallen. She looks like she's just about to faint when her husband shouts out from the back of courtroom, "She stole a can of peas, too!"

The couple had been dating for quite some time and the girl's birthday was coming up. "What would you like for your big day, sweetheart?"
"Surprise me with a diamond," she said.
So he gave her a deck of cards.

She Said: You've had way too much to drink!

He Said: My dear, you are ugly. Tomorrow I will be sober, but you will still be ugly.

Little Johnny greeted his grandmother with a big hug as she arrived.
"Gramma's here! Now Daddy will do that trick he promised!"
"What trick is that, Johnny?" asked his grandmother.
"Daddy said if you came to visit one more time this year he'd climb up a wall!"

A man finally escapes after being held hostage by kidnappers for seven years. He arrives home, filthy, exhausted and hungry. His wife says, "Where have you been? You escaped nine hours ago!"

She Said: I'm only going to tell you this one more time...

He Said: There's no need to repeat yourself. I ignored you just fine the first time.

"This past Christmas, I told my girlfriend that all I wanted was an Xbox. That's it. Beginning and end of list: Xbox. You know what she got me? A homemade frame with a picture of us from our first date together. Which was fine. Because I got her an Xbox." -Anthony Jeselnik

She Said: I thought you said you were going to mow the lawn.

He Said: I'm waiting on a part.

She Said: What part?

He Said: The part of me that wants to do it.

"One of the reasons ballet is so popular is that for two hours men can watch lovely women who never say a word." *-Bill Pereira*

"I once heard two ladies going on and on about the pains of childbirth and how men don't seem to know what real pain is. I asked if either of them ever got themselves caught in a zipper." *-Emo Philips*

One cannibal says to the other, "You know, I really don't care for my mother-in-law."
The other cannibal replies, "Just eat your vegetables then."

Morty and Fred were teeing off early one summer's day when the usual tranquility of the golf course was shattered by the siren of an ambulance racing to the maternity hospital atop a nearby hill.
"Somebody's getting a big surprise today," said Morty.
"I'll say," replied Fred as he lined up his putt. "When I left this morning, my wife's contractions were still at least an hour apart."

He Said: Will you dance with me?

She Said: I'm not gonna dance with a kid.

He Said: Sorry, I didn't realize you were pregnant.

"There's very little advice in men's magazines, because men don't think there's a lot they don't know. Women do. Women want to learn. Men think, 'I know what I'm doing, just show me somebody naked.'" -*Jerry Seinfeld*

"Kissing is just pushing your lips against the sweet end of 66 feet of intestines." -*Drew Carey*

"In a perfect world, no man, including the husband, would ever be invited to a baby shower." -*Jason Love*

The medium studied the crystal ball and said to the man, "I see a buried treasure."
He replied, "Yes, it's probably my wife's first husband."

Blind date conversation

She Said: Are you Elmer?

He Said: Are you Ethel?

She Said: Yeah.

He Said: Then I'm not Elmer.

He Said: Remember when I asked for your opinion?

She Said: No.

He Said: Me neither.

Q: What's the difference between a woman and a magnet?

A: Magnets have a positive side.

A guy goes into a bank and gets in line. When it's his turn, he pulls out a gun and demands all of the bank's money from the teller. After he gets all the loot, he wants to make sure there are no witnesses, so he turns to the next customer in line and says, "Did you see me rob this bank?"

When the customer nods, the robber shoots him. The robber points his gun at the next guy in line and says, "Did you see me rob the bank?"

The guy replies, "No, but my wife did."

A guy approached a beautiful woman in the supermarket and said, "Excuse me, but my wife and I got separated while we were shopping. Can I talk to you for a couple of minutes."

"Why?"

The guy answered, "Because every time I talk to a gorgeous woman, my wife appears out of nowhere."

"I don't have EX's! I have Y's. Like 'Y the hell did I date you?!'" -*Kevin Hart*

She Said: Do you have Facebook?

He Said: No.

She Said: Do you have Twitter?

He Said: No.

She Said: Do you have Instagram?

He Said: No.

She Said: Then what do you have!?!

He Said: A life.

One snowy morning, a husband and wife wake up and hear the latest forecast on the radio. "Five to six inches more of the white stuff is expected. Alternate side of the street parking is in effect. You can only park on the even numbered side of the street today, folks."

With that, the wife gets dressed, goes out and moves her car to the other side of the street.

A week later she hears a similar forecast. "Three to six inches expected this morning. Parking on only the odd numbered side of the street today."

The wife goes out and moves the car again.

A few days later comes this radio announcement: "We're going to be hit with a big snowstorm today. As far as parking goes..."

All of the sudden, the power is lost! The worried wife turns to her husband and says, "Now I don't know where to park my car. What should I do?"

The husband answers, "I'd say you should just leave it in the garage."

"I hate women because they always know where things are." *-James Thurber*

He Said: Hey babe, you smell that?

She Said: No.

He Said: Me neither, start cooking.

"If a woman tells you she's 20 and looks 16, she's 12. If she tells you she's 26 and looks 26, she's damn near 40." -*Chris Rock*

"My life today is tough. My wife, she's attached to a machine that keeps her alive - the refrigerator." -*Rodney Dangerfield*

"You know what blows my mind? Women can see breasts any time they want. You just look down, and there they are. How you get any work done is beyond me." -*Joey Tribbiani,* Friends

A man was riding a bicycle built for two all alone when he was pulled over by the police. "What's the problem, officer?" he asked.
"Perhaps you hadn't noticed but your wife fell off a half-mile back," the officer replied.
"Oh, thank God," the bicyclist said as he wiped his brow. "I was afraid that I had gone deaf!"

She Said: Do I look fat in this dress?

He Said: Do I look dumb in this shirt?

He Said: You know, we'd have less arguments if you wouldn't be so pedantic.

She Said: Fewer arguments.

"Women can do anything men can do… except math, chess, running, jumping, lifting stuff, fixing things, making money, hockey, surfing, driving, making decisions, being tall, taking out the garbage, tipping, fishing, being funny on purpose, reading a map, listening to good bands, writing, running the country, inventing anything important, or being fun to hang out with. Don't get me wrong, I love women. I just think they should drink from a separate water fountain." *-Daniel Tosh*

She Said: It's payday. How much did you bring home?

He Said: I already spent most of it on the house.

She Said: What? What could you possibly buy for the house that would cost so much?

He Said: Ten rounds of drinks.

A guy sat down at a bar and ordered rapid-fire drinks. The bartender asked him what was wrong. "I had a big fight with my wife and she said she wouldn't speak to me for a whole month."
Trying to look on the bright side, the bartender poured him another drink and said, "Well, maybe that's for the best. A little peace and quiet can do a guy a lot of good you know."
"Yeah," said the man. "But this is my last day!"

She Said: How would you describe me?

He Said: You are ABCDEFGHIJK.

She Said: What's that supposed to mean?

He Said: Adorable, beautiful, cute, delightful, elegant, first-class, gorgeous, and hot.

She Said: Aw, thank you... but what about IJK?

He Said: I'm just kidding!

Q: Why do men twist their wedding rings on their fingers?
A: They're trying to crack the combination.

Q: Did you hear about the cannibal who ate his mother-in-law?
A: She still disagreed with him.

"Rupert," the wife barked as her husband arrived home from work. "I want you to know that the huge, ugly cypress wood clock you had to lug back from Florida almost killed Mother today. She was sitting on the couch and had just gotten up when it fell from the wall right where she had been sitting seconds before."
"Sorry," Rupert groaned. "That lousy clock always was slow."

"Paying alimony is like feeding hay to a dead horse."
-Groucho Marx

She Said: Dear, if I died, would you remarry?

He Said: Well, I guess so. After all, we're not exactly senior citizens.

She Said: Would you live in this house with her?

He Said: I would think so.

She Said: How about my car? Would she get that?

He Said: I don't see why not.

She Said: What about my golf clubs? Would you give them to her, too?

He Said: Of course not. She's left-handed.

"What's the difference between my wife and a terrorist? You can negotiate with a terrorist."
-Frank Carson

"When a man gets close to a woman wearing a leather mini-skirt, his heart starts beating faster, his throat gets dry, his knees get weak and he becomes irrational. Why? Because the leather smells like a new car." *-Dan D'Aloia*

A guy staggers out of a bar and realizes he's in no shape to drive. He leaves his car there and starts to walk home. As he's stumbling along, a cop stops him and says, "What's up buddy?"
"I'm goin' to a lecture," slurs the guy.
"At two in the morning? Just who is giving a lecture at this hour?" asks the cop.
"My wife."

He Said: I've got a great weekend planned!

She Said: That's terrific, honey.

He Said: I'll see you Monday.

One night, Harry was working on his prized Porsche in the garage. His bride of five months was standing there watching him. At one point she said, "You know, now that we're married, maybe it's time you quit spending so many hours here in the garage. And maybe you should sell that car. While you're at it, you might want to get rid of your fishing gear- oh, and also that old baseball card collection. That way we can spend more time together."
Harry got a terribly distraught look on his face. His wife said, "Did I say something wrong?"
"Well," Harry responded, "you're beginning to sound a lot like my ex-wife."
"Ex-wife!? You never told me you were married before!"
Harry answered, "I wasn't."

Old Farnsworth was leaning over the bar, crying in his beer. "My wife says if I ever go fishin' again, she's going to leave me."
"Gee, that's tough," his friend commiserated.
"Yeah," sniffed Farnsworth, wiping a tear from his eye. "I'm sure going to miss her."

"I always look for a woman who has a tattoo. I see a woman with a tattoo and I'm thinking, 'Okay, here's a gal who's making a decision she'll regret in the future.'" -Richard Jeni

He Said: Two things- Number one: Where have you been all my life?

She Said: And number two?

He Said: Could you please go back there?

Q: How come only 5% of women go to Heaven?
A: Because if they all went, it would be Hell.

Lady Astor: Sir, if you were my husband, I would poison your drink.
Winston Churchill: Madam, if you were my wife, I would drink it.

"Ever get one of those ice cream headaches? You know, when you tell your girlfriend she's gaining weight, and she hits you with the scoop? 'Ow! I said that too fast!'" *-Jeff Shaw*

"My wife and I took out a life insurance policy on each other, so now it's just a waiting game."
-Bill Dwyer

A guy visiting his psychiatrist explained that a recent visit with his ex-girlfriend didn't go too well.
"What happened?" asked the shrink.
"Well, we were at the dinner table. I meant to say, 'Pass the salt, please,' but what I said was, 'You witch. You ruined my life!'"

She Said: I wouldn't marry you if you were the last person on Earth.

He Said: Good- then you won't be here.

"A bachelor is a man who never makes the same mistake once." *-Ed Wynn*

"I don't respect prostitutes. I think they've sold out." *-Craig Sharf*

At a nightclub...

He Said: Would you like to dance?

She Said: I wouldn't dance with you if you were the last person on Earth.

He Said: You misunderstood. I said you look fat in those pants.

A young brunette goes into the doctor's office and says that her body hurts wherever she touches it. "Show me," says the doctor.
She takes her finger and pushes her elbow and screams in agony. She touches her ankle and screams, then touches her knee and writhes in agony.
The doctor says, "You're not really a brunette are you?"
She says, "No, I'm a blonde."
"I thought so," he says. "Your finger is broken."

She Said: Sweetheart, what's the definition of divorce?

He Said: The future tense of marriage.

An elderly retired couple were discussing their future. "What will you do if I should die before you?" the husband asked.

The wife thought for a moment and replied, "Oh, I guess I'd look for a situation where I could share a place with two or three single or widowed women. I think I'd prefer them to be younger than I am since I'm still very active... What would you do if I die first?"

He replied, "I guess I'd do the same thing."

"My wife has a slight impediment in her speech. Every now and then she stops to breathe."
-Jimmy Durante

"A couple of months ago, I gave my girlfriend some fancy lingerie, and she actually got mad at me. She said, 'Anthony, I think this is more of a gift for you than it is for me.' And I said, 'If you want to get technical, it was originally a gift for my last girlfriend.'" *-Anthony Jeselnik*

"My wife is the sweetest, most tolerant, most beautiful woman in the world. This is a paid political announcement." *-Henny Youngman*

She Said: Tell me you don't only love me because of the fortune my father left me.

He Said: Of course not. I'd love you no matter who left you the money.

Son: Is it true, Dad, that in some parts of Africa a man doesn't know his wife until he marries her?
Dad: That happens in every country, son.

Hank, a 75-year-old, extremely wealthy widower, shows up at the golf club with a drop-dead gorgeous 30-year-old blonde. One of his buddies at the club pulls him aside and asks, "Hank, how did you manage to land that trophy girlfriend?"
Hank answers, "She's not my girlfriend. She's my wife."
Amazed, Hank's buddy asks, "How did you persuade her to marry you?"
"I lied about my age," Hank replies.
His buddy grins and says, "What'd you tell her- that you were only 50?"
"Nope. I told her I was 90."

"There is one thing I would break up over, and that is if she caught me with another woman. I wouldn't stand for that." *-Steve Martin*

She Said: I've got to shed a few pounds.

He Said: I wouldn't worry about it. You're just getting broad-shouldered around the hips.

She Said: I'm tired of arguing. One of these days, you're gonna be sorry! I'm going to leave you!

He Said: Make up your mind. Which one is it?

A small-town family of three was touring New York City and walked into the Empire State Building. The mother paused to view the magnificent art in the lobby while the father and son went on ahead and, for the first time in their lives, saw an elevator. They were perplexed by the sideways sliding doors and couldn't imagine what the little room was for. Just then, an elderly woman walked up and hit the button. The doors opened and she stepped in. The boy and his dad watched as the doors closed and the little round numbers went higher and higher. Then they paused and dropped back down. A little bell sounded, the doors opened and out stepped a voluptuous, 18-year-old beauty that any country boy would be proud to have as a kissin' cousin. The father was simply amazed and, keeping his eye on the elevator, tapped the boy on the shoulder. "Son," he said intently, "Go get your mother."

"Scientists now believe that the primary biological function of breasts is to make men stupid."
-Dave Barry

"I met a beautiful girl last night, but she was rather thin. I mean, this was a skinny girl. She turned sideways, you didn't see her. I took her to a restaurant and the maitre d' said to me, 'Check your umbrella?'" *-Mel Brooks*

She Said: If it weren't for my money, this house wouldn't be here!

He Said: If it weren't for your money, I wouldn't be here.

"When my wife says she'll be ready in five minutes I know I have just enough time to fly to space and write a poem on the moon before we go."
-Mike Vanatta

"I don't have a girlfriend. But I do know a woman who'd be mad at me for saying that."
-Mitch Hedberg

On the street corner in New York a vendor waved a bouquet at a passerby. "Take home a bundle for your wife, sir."
The passerby replied, "I'm not married."
"Then take a bundle for your sweetheart."
"I don't have a girlfriend, either."
"Well, then, take home a couple of bundles to celebrate!"

He Said: I love what you've done with your hair.

She Said: Why, thank you.

He Said: How do you get it to come out of your nostrils like that?

She Said: I'm not fat, am I?

He Said: Hang on just a minute. I'll walk over to your front side.

It was New Year's Eve. All the wives of the regulars of the local bar suggested that at the stroke of midnight every husband should stand next to the one person who made his life worth living.
The bartender was nearly crushed to death.

Little Johnny's in class. The teacher says, "For our English lesson today, we're going to talk about tenses- future tense, present tense and past tense. For instance, if I said 'I am beautiful,' what tense is that?"
Little Johnny raises his hand. The teacher says, "Yes, Johnny?"
Little Johnny says, "That would be past tense."

She Said: I think I'm putting on some weight.

He Said: Don't be silly, babe. You're not fat. You're just easy to see.

"The main reason Santa is so jolly is because he knows where all the bad girls live." -*George Carlin*

"Men don't settle down. Men surrender."
-*Chris Rock*

He Said: Where do you want to go for our anniversary?

She Said: Someplace I've never been before.

He Said: How about the kitchen?

"You ever hear girls say that 'I'm not religious, but I'm spiritual'? I like to reply with 'I'm not honest, but you're interesting!'" -*Daniel Tosh*

"If I get married again, I want a guy there with a drum to do rimshots during the vows." -*Sam Kinison*

"I got married to complicate my thought process. When you're single, you're brain is single-minded. Single guys think three things: 'I'd like to go out with her,' 'I'd like to buy one of those,' and 'I hope those guys win.'" -*Jerry Seinfeld*

An investigative reporter traveled to Afghanistan to study the ways of the people and was shocked to find that women were made to walk ten paces behind men. When she asked one of the local guides why this was so, he replied, "Because they are considered of lesser status."
The reporter was outraged and greatly disturbed by this, but a year later when she returned to cover another story, she was surprised to see the women walking ten paces ahead of the men. She asked her guide, "What's changed in a year's time?"
The guide answered, "Land mines."

She Said: Sweetheart, do you think I'm putting on weight?

He Said: No, the living room just got smaller.

A married couple were in a horrible accident where the wife's face was severely burned. The doctor told her that they couldn't graft skin from her body because she was too thin. The husband offered to donate some of his own skin and the doctor advised that it would have to come from his buttocks. Arrangements were made for the operation, the surgery took place and the result was a resounding success. The wife looked as radiant as ever, her face revealing not one iota of the ordeal she'd experienced.

She was overcome with emotion and said to her husband, "Dear, I can't possibly thank you enough for the sacrifice you made."

"Honey," he answered, "I get all the thanks I need every time I see your mother kiss you on the cheek."

Frick: I'm in big trouble with my girlfriend. She showed the engagement ring I gave her to the girls at work.

Frack: Didn't they admire it?

Frick: Admire it? Half of them recognized it.

She Said: If you won the lottery, would you leave me?

He Said: Of course not. I'd need someone to do my new girlfriend's laundry.

He Said: Sweetheart, our 25th (anniversary) is coming up. Tell me what you'd like. I'll spare no expense.

She Said: I'd like a divorce.

He Said: To tell you the truth, I wasn't thinking of spending quite that much.

"We men are driven to meet Miss Right … or at least Miss Right Now." *-Robin Williams*

"My friends actually set me up on blind dates. When you see the girl, you want to jab something sharp into your eyeballs." *-Kevin Meaney*

"My wife dresses to kill. She cooks the same way." *-Henny Youngman*

"The first thing men notice about a woman is her eyes. Then, when her eyes aren't looking, they notice her breasts." *-Conan O'Brien*

Edith was fuming as her husband, Oswald, staggered through the front door. There was alcohol on his breath and lipstick on his collar.
"I am going to take a leap of faith and say that there's a very good reason for you to come traipsing home at 7:30 in the morning," she growled.
"Yes," Oswald said. "Breakfast."

She Said: Honey, if we get engaged, will you give me a ring?

He Said: Sure. What's your phone number?

An old guy crashed his cart into a younger man's cart at one of those huge bulk-buy warehouses.
"Oh, I'm sorry," said the old man. "I was distracted. You see I've been trying to find my wife for the past half-hour."
"I know how you feel," said the younger man. "I've been looking for mine for 45 minutes and I'm getting a bit concerned."
"Well maybe we can help each other out," the old man said. "What's your wife look like?"
"She's 23, fantastic figure, green eyes, red hair and the prettiest face you've ever seen," the young man replied. "What's your wife look like?"
"Never mind that," the old guy replied. "Let's just look for yours."

Q: How many men does it take to open a beer?
A: None. It should be opened by the time she brings it.

Q: Why do women have smaller feet than men?
A: It allows them to stand closer to the kitchen sink.

"For the sake of your marriage, get a king-size bed. And if you really want to stay married, get two."
-Ray Romano

She Said: You twist everything I say to your advantage!

He Said: I take that as a compliment.

At his 50th wedding anniversary party held at the local country club, Ralph was asked the secret of his long marriage. He stood up before his assembled crowd of friends and relatives and shared his marital philosophy.

"Gertrude and I have made it a practice throughout our long marriage to play golf and then go out for two romantic, candlelit dinners a week right here at this country club. Unfailingly, twice a week, we come here and enjoy the delicious food and soft music. We soak up the ambiance of this fine establishment and sip a vintage wine. She goes Thursdays and I go Fridays."

It's St. Patrick's Day and he's just proposed to her:

She Said: You cheap bum. This isn't even real.

He Said: I know, but in honor of St. Patrick, I decided to buy you a sham rock.

"If it can't be fixed by duct-tape or WD-40, it's a female problem." *-Jason Love*

"You know that look women get when they want sex? Me neither." *-Steve Martin*

She Said: How much do you love me?

He Said: Look at the stars and count them. That's how much I love you.

She Said: But it's morning.

He Said: Exactly.

"I never mind my wife having the last word; in fact, I'm delighted when she gets to it." -*Walter Matthau*

"I've often wanted to drown my troubles, but I can't get my wife to go swimming." -*Jimmy Carter*

"My wife got pulled over for making an 'S' turn. She started to make a 'U,' then changed her mind." -*Gabe Abelson*

Q: Why does a blonde nurse carry around a red pen?
A: To draw blood.

Q: What's the definition of a confirmed bachelor?
A: A man who never Mrs. a woman.

Did you hear about the new 12 step program for women that talk too much?
It's called Onandonandon.

She Said: What do you like most in me- my beautiful face or my sexy body?

He Said: Your sense of humor.

Two buddies met at a bar and one asked the other how things were going.
"Not so hot- had an argument with the wife," was his answer.
"What happened?" asked his friend sympathetically.
"We had money troubles so she told me I couldn't buy beer by the case anymore. Then I caught her paying $50 a bottle for nail polish off a TV shopping channel."
"That's not right."
"Yeah, and then she went to a beauty parlor and had a $200 makeover."
"So what'd you do?"
"I confronted her and demanded to know why she was wasting all that money."
"What did she say?"
"She said that she had to. She needed all that stuff so that she could look prettier for me."
"What'd you say?"
"I said 'Are you crazy? That's what the beer was for in the first place.'"

"She got her good looks from her father. He's a plastic surgeon." -*Groucho Marx*

"Women are like the police. They could have all the evidence in the world but they still want the confession." -*Chris Rock*

She Said: Am I pretty or ugly?

He Said: You're both.

She Said: What does that mean?

He Said: You're pretty ugly.

"I'm going to be 50 this year. Soon I'm going to meet somebody around my own age, and she's going to be smart and beautiful, and I'm going to date her daughter." *-Bob Saget*

"There are more men than women in mental hospitals - which just goes to show who's driving who crazy." *-Peter Veale*

A woman woke up on Valentine's Day and said to her husband, "Dear, I had a dream that you bought me the most beautiful diamond necklace. I wonder what that means."
The husband replied, "You'll soon find out."
That night, he came home with her Valentine's gift. She opened up the present and found a book titled *The Meaning of Dreams*.

She Said: What are you doing?

He Said: Nothing.

She Said: Nothing? You've been reading our marriage certificate for half an hour.

He Said: I was looking for the expiration date.

She Said: You think we might get back together again?

He Said: Chances are probably better of me putting Super Unleaded in a rented car.

"Ladies ask the craziest things. My last girlfriend, all quiet, she turned to me and would be like, 'Would you still love me if I weighed 500 lbs?' I was like, 'Why- is that one of your goals?'"
-*Michael Somerville*

"My wife had us register for fine china, because you never know when the Pope is going to swing by and want a microwaved hot dog on a $200 plate."
-*Jim Gaffigan*

Q: Why can't you tell women knock-knock jokes?
A: Because they always leave to answer the door.

Late one night a trucker walked into a diner, plopped down on the stool and put a $100 bill down on the counter. "The Ben Franklin is yours," he said to the manager, "if you get me an overcooked cheeseburger served by your ugliest waitress."
"But for that kind of money you can have a well-cooked, seven course meal and take plenty of snacks for the road," said the manager.
The trucker would have none of that, replying, "I'm not hungry. I'm homesick."

He Said: I can't believe you're dumping me at two in the morning through a text.

She Said: I'm sorry. Can I come get my stuff?

He Said: Yes, it's on the grill.

She Said: On the grill?!? Why?

He Said: I ran out of charcoal.

A guy was walking on the sidewalk when he heard a voice say, "Stop! Stop! If you take one more step, a brick will fall down on your head."
The fellow stopped short and a brick fell right in front of him.
He continued on to a crosswalk and just as he was about to step into the street the voice again shouted, "Stop! If you take one more step, a car will run you over."
The man took a step back just as a car came speeding around the corner and barely missed him.
"Who are you and where are you?" the guy asked.
"I am your guardian angel," replied the voice.
"Is that so?" said the man. "And where, may I ask, were you when I got married?"

My wife is so negative. I remembered the car seat, the stroller, AND the diaper bag. Yet all she can talk about is how I forgot the baby.

"Some women (and here I'm referring to my wife) can share as many as three days' worth of feelings about an event that took eight seconds to actually happen." *-Dave Barry*

She Said: I'm ready now.

He Said: Gimme a couple of minutes.

She Said: I thought you said you were ready a long time ago.

He Said: I was. I've gotta shave again.

Little Johnny asks his mother her age. She replies, "Gentlemen don't ask a lady how old she is." Johnny then asks his mother how much she weighs. His mother once again answers, "Gentlemen don't ask ladies that question." Johnny then asks, "Why did Daddy leave you?" His mother says, "You shouldn't ask that." A bit later, Johnny gets into some mischief. Rummaging through his mother's purse, he comes across her driver's license. He runs up to his mother and excitedly says, "I know all about you now. You're 35 years old, you weigh 125 pounds and Daddy left you because you got an 'F' in sex!"

She Said: We've been really busy at the checkout today, sir. I'm sorry about your wait.

He Said: You're not too skinny, yourself.

"Man does not control his own fate. The women in his life do that for him." *-Groucho Marx*

"We've been married three months. I'm just not used to being wrong so often." *-Dennis Regan*

She Said: Do you love me?

He Said: Yes, dear.

She Said: Would you die for me?

He Said: No... Mine is an undying love.

Ralph forgot his wedding anniversary and his wife was more than a bit agitated. "Tomorrow morning, I expect to find a gift in the driveway that goes from 0 to 200 in five seconds. And it better be there or else!" she yelled.

The next morning Ralph woke up early to do his thing. When his wife got up, she looked out the window and sure enough there was a gift-wrapped box, smack in the middle of the driveway. The wife put on her robe and slippers, ran outside and opened it up right then and there- a bathroom scale.

"I met my wife in a bar. What a surprise! I thought she was home watching the kids." *-Ron Dentinger*

"My last girlfriend had a memory so good she could remember things that never happened."
-Greg Tamblyn

"Women will gab at each other for 57 hours, breaking down every emotional thing they're going through into nuances. A man will sit down with his buddy and his buddy will ask, 'What's up with your wife?' The man will mumble, 'Oh, man, she's tripping.' End of analysis." *-Sinbad*

She Said: I often laugh about how competitive we are.

He Said: Yes, and I laugh more.

The boss is in the middle of interviewing a managerial candidate and decides it's time for a character check. He says to the guy, "Let's assume that you go to my house and my wife invites you in, but tells you that I won't be home for another few hours. What would you do?"
The job applicant thinks for a moment and says, "Would you mind showing me a picture of her?"

Oliver arrived home and told his wife, "I have a friend coming over for dinner."
"What?" his wife protested. "My hair is in curlers, the house is a mess, the kids are particularly noisy and wild and I was only going to serve something out of a box. Why on earth would you invite him over?"
"Because," Oliver replied, "He's thinking of getting married."

She Said: All men are the same.

He Said: Who asked you to try all of them?

"The only marriage I've observed for any length of time is my parents- 35 years. I asked my pop, I go, 'Pop, 35 years- what do you hope for?' He's like, 'I hope you die first.'" *-Adam Ferrara*

He Said: Babe, when I got my draft notice, you were right by my side. When I totaled my car, you were there. When my business went south, you were there. Now that I'm dying, here you are, right by my bedside. You know what, babe?

She Said: What's that, dear?

He Said: I think you're bad luck.

"The problem with life is, by the time you can read women like a book, your library card has expired." *-Milton Berle*

"Before you marry a person, you should first make them use a computer with slow Internet service to see who they really are." *-Will Ferrell*

Clem: You know, it's times like this when I wished I listened to what my wife told me.
Herb: What did she say?
Clem: I have no clue. I wasn't listening.

Milton walked into a bar when he saw his buddy Merv downing one shot after another. "What's going on here?" Milton demanded.
"My wife ran off with my best friend!" Merv exclaimed.
"Hey, wait a second!" said Mark. "I thought I was your best friend."
"Not anymore," Merv said with a drunken smile. "He is!"

She Said: You don't like any of my relatives.

He Said: Not true. I like your mother-in-law better than I like mine.

Gertrude's car was pelted in a driving hailstorm one night, resulting in hundreds of dents. The next day she visits a body shop to get it fixed. The repairman figures he'll have a little fun with her and tells Gertrude that all she has to do is blow into the exhaust pipe really hard and the dents will pop out. Gertrude goes home and blows furiously into the tailpipe. When her blonde roommate asks what Gertrude's doing, she explains what the repairman advised her to do. "But it doesn't work," she says. "Hellooo," says the blonde. "You gotta roll up the windows first."

She Said: What would you like for dinner?

He Said: Let's eat out tonight and give the smoke detector a rest.

"We sleep in separate rooms, we have dinner apart, we have separate vacations - we're doing everything we can to keep our marriage together."
-Rodney Dangerfield

"All men make mistakes, but married men find out about them sooner." *-Red Skelton*

He Said: I'm going to treat you like royalty tonight.

She Said: Sounds exciting. Where are we going?

He Said: Burger King.

A guy was visiting his hunting buddy and saw a stuffed lion in his den. "Wow! When did you bag him?" the guy said.
"Two years ago when I went hunting with my wife," was the reply.
"What's he stuffed with?" asked the visitor.
"My wife."

Son: Hey, Dad. I got a part in the school play!
Father: What role do you play?
Son: The husband.
Father: Too bad they didn't give you a speaking part.

Q: How many jokes about women are there?
A: Just this one. All the rest are true.

Q: What do you call an Italian hooker?
A: A pasta-tute

"A woman won't dump a man until she's found someone to replace him. In a woman's mind, if you cheat on her, it's because you're a jerk. But if she cheats on you, it's because you're a jerk."
-Jeff Shaw

She Said: You're late and you're half-drunk. You've got some explaining to do.

He Said: It's not my fault. I ran out of money.

Wally took his mother-in-law by complete surprise when he presented her with a delicately scented, beautifully wrapped birthday gift. She unwrapped the present and opened the box to find a beautiful pair of earrings and a loaded handgun.
"Why, Wally, these are really gorgeous, but why the gun?"
"That's to pierce your ears with."

Q: What's the difference between a new wife and a new dog?
A: After a year, the dog is still excited to see you.

Q: Why did the polygamist cross the aisle?
A: To get to the other bride.

Q: What's the difference between a bachelor and a married man?
A: A bachelor comes home, sees what's in the fridge, and goes to bed. A married man arrives home, sees what's in bed, and goes to the fridge.

"Valentine's Day... or, as men like to call it: Extortion Day." *-Jay Leno*

She Said: You know, if something ever happened to you, I don't think I could every marry again.

He Said: I know what you mean. Once is enough.

I asked my girlfriend what she wanted for her birthday. She told me, "Nothing would make her happier than a diamond ring."
So I bought her nothing.

If a woman is in the forest, talking to herself with no man around, is she still complaining?

"There's a way of transferring funds that is even faster than electronic banking. It's called marriage."
-Sam Kinison

"I love being married. I was single for a long time, and I just got so sick of finishing my own sentences." *-Brian Kiley*

He Said: I have one last request before I die, dear.

She Said: Of course, anything you wish.

He Said: A few months after I die, I want you to marry Harry.

She Said: But I thought you hated Harry.

He Said: I do.

He Said: What's the matter, honey?

She Said: I made your dinner and the dog ate it.

He Said: No problem, dear. I'll get you another dog.

A guy desperately wants to go to the Super Bowl, so he seeks out a scalper but is only able to get one ticket. He pays top dollar for a seat in the nose-bleed section, the second to last row of the upper deck. As the game begins, the guy's watching through his binoculars. He notices that there's an empty seat in the very first row, right on the 50-yard line. As the second quarter is about to end, he looks down and sees that the 50-yard line seat is still empty. At halftime, he makes his way down to the empty seat and asks the guy who's sitting in the next seat, "Is this taken?"
The guy replies, "No."
"Would you mind if I sit here?"
The other guy says, "Not at all. Go right ahead."
"I wonder why someone with a front row, 50-yard line seat wouldn't show up at the Super Bowl," says the first guy.
The second guy says, "Actually, my wife and I have come to every Super Bowl since 1967, but she passed away."
"Oh, gee, I'm sorry to hear that," says the first guy. "But couldn't you get a friend or relative to come to the game?"
"I tried to, but they're all at the funeral."

"The only difference between the women I've dated and Charles Manson is that Manson has the decency to look like a nut case when you first meet him."
-Richard Jeni

He Said: You know, dear, it's nice that you treat me like an idol at dinner.

She Said: Why do you say that?

He Said: You feed me burnt offerings.

A dietician is conducting a seminar before a huge crowd. He tells the folks, "Much of the food we eat today is extremely unhealthful. Red meat is dangerous. Many vegetables are sprayed with pesticides and are unsafe. Drinking water can be contaminated. However, there is one food that is far and away the most dangerous of all. Can anyone tell me what it is?"
Following a long pause, a man in the back sticks his hand up and yells, "Wedding cake!"

In the beginning God created the Earth and rested. Then God created Man and rested. Then God created Woman. Since then, neither God nor Man has rested.

A married couple are at a wishing well. The husband throws in a penny and makes a wish. The wife goes to do the same, but leans over too far and falls in. The husband looks deep down into the well and says, "Wow, it really works!"

"Women are like elephants to me: nice to look at, but I wouldn't want to own one." *-W.C. Fields*

He Said: I think I like this girl…

She Said: Really? Who is that?

He Said: Well, she kinda looks like you.

She Said: Aww… Is it me?

He Said: No, your sister.

As the casket is being carried out after a woman's funeral service, the pallbearers bump into a wall. The husband hears a faint moan, opens the casket and finds out that his wife is still alive!

Ten years later, the woman dies "again" and another funeral is held. At the end of the service, as the casket is being carried toward the door, the husband shouts, "Watch out for the wall!"

She Said: I need my beauty sleep.

He Said: Sorry, Sweetie, but with your looks, I think you need to hibernate.

"My first wife, I'll never forget her - and I've tried." -Redd Foxx

"My girlfriend said she wanted me to tease her. I said, 'Alright, fatty.'" -Jimmy Carr

"Best wishes for a happy and successful first marriage." -Marc Rosen

He Said: Were you born on the highway?

She Said: No, why?

He Said: Cuz that's where most accidents happen.

Two guys are talking in a bar when one says to the other, "My mother-in-law is an angel."
His friend replies, "You're lucky. Mine is still alive."

A woman's husband comes home hammered every night, and she always yells at him before going to bed alone. One day she decides to try some reverse psychology. When her husband staggers in that night, she's waiting for him in her best lingerie. She sits him in an armchair and gives him a back rub. "It's getting late, big boy," she says after a few minutes. "Why don't we go upstairs to bed?"
"We might as well," slurs the husband. "I'm going to be in trouble when I get home, anyway."

"I'm dating a homeless woman. It was easier to talk her into staying over." *-Garry Shandling*

"My wife said to me, 'I want to be cremated.' I said, 'How about Tuesday?'" *-Buddy Hackett*

She Said: You never listen to me.

He Said: What?

She Said: Haven't you ever seen a bikini before? Stop staring at me!

He Said: I'm only looking at the covered parts.

"Women should be obscene and not heard."
-Groucho Marx

"Marriage is really tough because you have to deal with feelings *and* lawyers." *-Richard Pryor*

"Until Eve arrived, this was a man's world."
-Roy Harry

Any married man should forget his mistakes. There's no use in two people remembering the same thing.

A couple was asked to individually write a sentence using the words "love" and "sex."
The woman's sentence read, "When two people love each other, it is morally acceptable to engage in the practice of sex."
The guy wrote, "I love sex."

My sweetheart told me I should be more affectionate. So now I have two girlfriends.

She Said: Do you realize what you did!?

He Said: No, but I'll admit I'm wrong. What did I do?

Down in the canyons of Wall Street, a fabulously wealthy stockbroker passed a bedraggled beggar dressed in rags.

"Please, sir, may I trouble you for a dollar so that I might get a bite to eat?" pleaded the beggar.

"You poor fellow," said the stockbroker. "Come with me and I'll buy you a drink."

"Actually, sir, I don't drink, but I would like a bite to eat."

"Here, my good man. Take one of my special stock of Cuban cigars," urged the broker.

"Sorry, sir," said the bum. "I don't smoke."

"Then come with me down to Atlantic City. I'll stake you in the casino and you might win enough to get your life back on track."

"I can't do that, sir. I don't gamble, but I would still like a bite to eat."

"You want to eat?" asked the stockbroker. "Very well, come home with me and have dinner with us."

"Thank you. You're very kind, sir."

"Not at all," replied the broker. "I just want my wife to see what happens to a man who doesn't drink, smoke or gamble."

"My best friend ran away with my wife. I really miss him." *-Henny Youngman*

She Said: I feel like taking a moonlight walk.

He Said: Great idea. Take the dog with you.

She Said: I could make you the happiest man on Earth.

He Said: You're leaving so soon?

Q: Why is a laundromat a really bad place to pick up a woman?
A: Because a woman who can't even afford a washing machine will probably never be able to support you.

Q: How do you know when a woman is about to say something smart?
A: When she begins with, "A man once told me...."

Q: How do you fix a woman's watch?
A: You don't. There's a clock over the oven.

Q: How come blonde jokes are so short?
A: So brunettes can remember them

Q: What do you have when your mother-in-law drives off a cliff in your brand new Mercedes?
A: Mixed emotions

"If variety is the spice of life, marriage is the big can of leftover Spam." *-Johnny Carson*

She Said: You always say I talk too much.

He Said: It's not that. I just love the sound you make when you shut up.

A guy was jumping on the train tracks yelling, "14, 14, 14, 14!"
A blonde happened to pass by, thought it looked like fun, and jumped on the tracks too, yelling, "14, 14, 14, 14!"
A train approached and the guy jumped off the tracks. The blonde got hit.
The guy jumped back on the tracks and shouted, "15, 15, 15, 15!"

A drunk walks into a bar, scouts out the place and sees a good-looking woman. He goes over to her and plants a kiss right on her lips. She's stunned at first, but when she recovers, she hauls off and slaps him. He says, "Oh, I'm sorry. I thought you were my Mrs. You look just like her."
The woman says, "You're worthless, you no-good drunk!"
He says, "And you sound like her, too."

"If you want to read about love and marriage, you've got to buy separate books." -*Alan King*

She Said: What would it take for you to go on a second honeymoon?

He Said: A second wife.

She Said: That couple next door are so sweet. Every morning he leaves and kisses her goodbye. And when he comes home at night, he almost always brings her flowers. Why can't you do that?

He Said: I don't even know her.

"Why doesn't your mother like me?" a girl asks her boyfriend.
"Oh, don't take it personally," he says. "She's never liked anyone I've brought home. I once dated someone almost exactly like her, and that was a disaster."
"What happened?"
"My father couldn't stand her."

A guy called his mother and said, "Ma, I just met the most beautiful girl. I think I'm in love already. What should I do?"
"Simple. Send her flowers and, on the card, invite her to your place for a home-cooked meal!"
A day later, the guy's mother called to see how the date had gone.
"Miserable," groaned her son.
"Didn't she come over?"
"Oh, she came over alright," said the son, "but she refused to cook."

"I'm all for women who get plastic surgery. Because plastic surgery allows you to make your outer appearance resemble your inner appearance - fake."
-Daniel Tosh

He Said: Babe, I just won the lottery!!! Pack up your things!

She Said: Great!! Shall I pack for warm weather or cold?

He Said: Doesn't matter to me. Just get the heck out!

"Just think, if it weren't for marriage, men would go through life thinking they had no faults at all."
-Henny Youngman

"I snore at night, so I bought a bunch of those Breathe Right Strips for my wife to shove in her ears." *-Guy Endore-Kaiser*

If a man is talking in the forest, and no woman is there to hear him, is he still wrong?

A wife was so furious at her husband that she packed his bags and told him to leave. As he walked toward the door she yelled, "I hope you die a long, slow, painful death."
He turned around and said, "So, you want me to stay?"

She Said: Are you talking back to me?

He Said: Yes, that's how a conversation works.

He Said: You look like my fifth wife.

She Said: Fifth wife!? How many have you had?

He Said: Four.

Charlie took his wife and mother-in-law to the Holy Land. While they were visiting Jerusalem, his mother-in-law suddenly dropped dead. He went to the American Consulate to make arrangements. "Shipping a body back to the States is a very expensive business," the consul warned. "It can cost upwards of $10,000. But if you bury the body here it's only about $300."
"Hmm," Charlie rubbed his chin and thought for a moment, "No, I'm having her shipped home no matter how much it costs. Someone rose from the dead here once before and I'm just not willing to take that chance."

If you want to find out who loves you more, stick your wife and dog in the trunk of your car for an hour or so. When you open the trunk, who is happy to see you?

She Said: Act your age.

He Said: I can't help it. I've never been this old before.

"A man's face is his autobiography. A woman's face is her work of fiction." *-Oscar Wilde*

He Said: Do you kiss on the first date?

She Said: No.

He Said: How about on the last date?

A husband and wife have been shopping for hours when the wife notices that her spouse has disappeared. She calls him on his cell phone and say, "Where have you gone?"
He responds, "Darling, you know that jewelry store where I promised you I'd buy you that gorgeous diamond necklace you always wanted?"
She excitedly answers, "Yes, dear! Yes!!"
He says, "Well, I'm having a beer at the bar next door."

Did you hear the one about the blonde who saw a sign in the ladies room that said "Employees Must Wash Hands"? She waited and waited all evening for one to come but finally had to do it herself.

When blondes have more fun, do they know it?

Waiter: How do you like your steak, sir?
Customer: Like winning an argument with my wife.
Waiter: Rare it is.

"Here's the secret to a happy marriage: Do what your wife tells you." -*Denzel Washington*

He Said: I have a magic watch. And it tells me that you're not wearing any panties.

She Said: I am so!

He Said: Oh no- It's an hour fast again.

"Arguing with a woman is like getting arrested. Everything you say can, and will, be used against you... So use your right to remain silent!"
-*Walter (the dummy of ventriloquist Jeff Dunham)*

A guy goes for a job at the CIA. The interviewer says, "So you want to be an agent?"
He replies, "I'd do anything to work for the CIA."
The CIA representative hands him a revolver and says, "Alright, go in the next room where your wife is waiting and shoot her."
The applicant hems and haws and says, "I can't do that. She's my partner for the rest of my life. I guess I'll have to pass on the CIA job."
A second man comes in for an interview. After a few questions, the CIA representative hands him a gun, too, and says, "If you really want to be an agent, go in the next room and shoot your wife."
The man responds, "No way. She's the love of my life and the mother of my three children."
A third applicant is given the same instructions, walks into the next room and closes the door. Gunshots ring out followed by the sounds of tables being overturned and lamps crashing. Finally, the applicant emerges and the interviewer says, "What happened in there?"
The wannabe agent replies, "The gun had blanks in it. I had to strangle her."

He Said: Would you like to dance?

She Said: Not with you.

He Said: Oh, c'mon. Lower your standards a little bit. I just did.

"Women aren't confusing. They're a Sudoku-Jenga puzzle surrounded by Rubik's cubes strapped to a terrorist screaming at you in another language."
-Mike Vanatta

"My wife gets so jealous. She came home from work and was mad at me because there was a pretty girl on the bus she thought I would have liked."
-Ray Romano

A woman is at the supermarket checkout counter with one bar of soap, one pint of milk, one single serving of cereal, one TV dinner and one can of Soup for One. The cashier says, "You're single, aren't you?"
She sarcastically says, "How could you possibly have guessed?"
He replies, "Because you're ugly."

A widow dies and goes to heaven. She sees her husband and runs up to him. Teary-eyed, she exclaims, "Oh, sweetheart. How I've missed you!" The husband steps back before she has a chance to embrace him and says, "Hold on there, woman. The contract was until death."

He Said: You know, you're living proof that nothing is impossible.

She Said: Awww… How so?

He Said: You do it every day.

I visited my wife's grave earlier today. A fellow walked by and said, "Morning."
I said, "No, just walking the dog."

My girlfriend left a note on the fridge that said, "It's not working. I can't take it anymore. I'm going to my mom's."
I opened the fridge door. The light came on. The beer was cold. What the hell did she mean?

He Said: I hear you're getting a divorce.

She Said: That's right.

He Said: Who's the lucky guy?

"Marriage is like a game of chess. Except the board is flowing water, the pieces are made of smoke and no move you make will have any effect on the outcome." *-Jerry Seinfeld*

"When you're in love, it's the most glorious two-and-a-half minutes of your life." *-Richard Lewis*

She Said: It's going to be our Silver Anniversary. Will you still love me when I turn grey?

He Said: Why not? I stuck with you through the other five shades.

"Here's all you have to know about men and women: women are crazy, men are stupid. And the main reason women are crazy is that men are stupid." -*George Carlin*

"I've had bad luck with both my wives. The first one left me, and the second one didn't." -*Patrick Murray*

"Marriage is not a word, but a sentence."
-*Mike Sauter*

Amos and Barney are downing a few at the local watering hole. Amos says, "I been thinkin' about divorcing my woman. She ain't spoken to me in almost three months."
"You better think twice about that," says Barney.
"Those women are hard to come by."

He Said: Do you have a boyfriend?

She Said: Yes.

He Said: That's okay. I'm not the jealous type.

She Said: I'm so upset. I've become so fat. I could use a compliment.

He Said: You've got perfect eyesight.

A guy goes to a police station to file a report on his missing wife. The officer filling out the report asks the husband to describe her.

"Alright," says the hubby, "but on one condition. You can't show her the report afterward."

Ollie: My wife's on a three-week diet.
Wally: Oh yeah? How much has she lost so far?
Ollie: Two weeks.

And then there was the guy whose television set was broken so he was forced to rely on the lost art of conversation with his beautiful bride. He said, "Have you seen the iPad, babe?"

If your dog is barking at the back door and your wife is yelling at the front door, which one of them do you let in first? The dog, naturally. He'll shut up once you let him in.

"A lot of people wonder how you know if you're really in love. Just ask yourself this one question: 'Would I mind being financially destroyed by this person?'" *-Ronnie Shakes*

She Said: Why does everything have to be a game with you?

He Said: An excellent question, my dear. But next time, please use the buzzer.

"This girl was fat. I hit her with my car. She asked me, 'Why didn't you go around me?' I told her, 'I didn't have enough gas.'" *-Rodney Dangerfield*

"A good wife always forgives her husband when she's wrong." *-Milton Berle*

"Men who don't understand women fall into two groups- bachelors and husbands." *-Geoff Scowcroft*

"My blind date arrived. She looks like something I'd draw with my left hand." *-Anonymous right-hander*

My wife said she wanted some peace and quiet while she cooked dinner. So I took out the batteries in the smoke alarm.

Fred: My dog bit my mother-in-law yesterday and I had to take him to the vet.
Frank: To be put down?
Fred: No- to have his teeth sharpened.

She Said: Before we met, you told me you were well off.

He Said: Yeah, and I didn't know just how well off.

An inebriated mathematician arrives home at three in the morning. His highly-agitated wife yells, "You're late. You said you'd be home no later than 11:45!" The mathematician answers, "My dear, I am precisely on time. I believe I said I'd be home by a quarter of twelve."

A pair of elderly couples were chatting at dinner when one of the husbands said, "Bentley, how was that memory clinic you went to last week?"
"Great," answered Bentley. "We were taught all the latest and greatest memory helpers - association, visualization - that kind of stuff."
"Sounds good... I might like to take a class. What was the name of it?"
Bentley's mind went blank. Then he suddenly smiled and said, "What do you call that flower that's red with a long stem and thorns?"
His buddy said, "You mean a rose?"
Bentley said, "Yeah, that's it," then turned to his wife and asked, "What was the name of that memory clinic, Rose?"

She Said: I should have married the devil instead of you!

He Said: You would have been arrested. It's illegal to marry relatives in this country.

She Said: How do I compare to your past girlfriends?

He Said: You're the only one I've ever been with…All the others were eights and nines.

"You know what I did before I married? Anything I wanted to." *-Henny Youngman*

"The reason God made man before woman was because he didn't want any suggestions."
-Sam Levenson

Herb and his wife were at a fancy restaurant when he noticed that his better half kept staring at an inebriated fellow a couple of tables away.
"That's disgusting. Look at him. He's drunk as a skunk," the wife complained.
"Do you know him?" asked Herb.
"Of course I do," the wife answered. "That's my ex. He's been drinking like that ever since I left him ten years ago."
"Holy cow!" exclaimed Herb. "I didn't know anybody could celebrate that long!"

The NFL season is just about to kick off…

He Said: Hey, babe.

She Said: Yes, dear?

He Said: Is there anything you wanted to say before the football season starts?

He Said: Would you like to go out with me?

She Said: I'd only go out with you on a day that doesn't end in "Y."

He Said: Great! I'll pick you up tomorrow.

A blonde has terribly sharp pains in her side, so she goes to the emergency room at the hospital. The doctor examines her and says, "You have acute appendicitis."
The blonde says, "That's sweet, Doc, but I came here for medical help."

A blonde calls American Airlines. She asks, "How long are your flights from New York to Rome?"
The airline telephone receptionist says, "Just a minute..."
The blonde says, "Thanks!" and hangs up the phone.

The burial service for the woman climaxed with a massive clap of thunder and a bolt of lightning.
"Well," said her husband to the mourners, "she's there."

"Women...can't live with 'em...pass the beer nuts."
-Norm Peterson, Cheers

"Behind every great man is a woman rolling her eyes." *-Jim Carrey*

She Said: Honey, as I text you, please send me your love. If you're sleeping, send me your dreams. If you're laughing, send me a smile. If you're drinking, think of me with each sip. I love you.

He Said: I'm on the toilet. Please advise.

Q: What did the cannibal say as he took his spouse's thigh out of the refrigerator?
A: Today is the first day of the rest of my wife.

Q: Why did God create Adam first?
A: So he'd have a chance to talk before Eve arrived.

Q: What do a Slinky and your mother-in-law have in common?
A: They're both a lot of fun to watch tumble down stairs.

"Mother in law" anagram- Woman Hitler

"I don't worry about terrorism. I was married for two years." *-Sam Kinison*

"I don't have a girlfriend, but sometimes I like to pretend I do. I just stand in my apartment screaming 'No, that's not what I said!'" *-Dave Attell*

He Said,
She Said

This Side For Women Only
(Joking About Men)

———— • ————

by

Jackie Kreismer

RED-LETTER PRESS, INC.
Saddle River, New Jersey

ACKNOWLEDGMENTS

EDITORIAL:
Jeff Kreismer

•

BOOK DESIGN & TYPOGRAPHY:
Jeff Kreismer

•

COVER ART:
Andrew Towl

•

CONTRIBUTORS:
Pat Pereira
Alix Perrault
David Reyneke
Kobus Reyneke
Mike Ryan
Jennifer Tomlinson

Red-Letter Press, Inc.
P.O. Box 393
Saddle River, NJ 07458

www.Red-LetterPress.com

He Said,
She Said

He Said: Your place or mine, babe?

She Said: Both. You go to yours and I'll go to mine.

An elderly couple in their nineties bickered all the time. Whenever there was an argument, the old man could be heard late into the night. Often he would threaten, "When I die, I'll dig my way up and out of the grave and come back to haunt you!"
The wife feared him. So did the neighbors. One night, the old man died. After he was buried, one of the neighbors who was concerned for the wife's safety said, "Aren't you afraid he might be able to dig his way out of the grave and haunt you for the rest of your life?"
The wife said, "He can dig all he wants. I had him buried upside down- and I know he won't ask for directions."

While creating men, God told women that a good and ideal man could be found in all corners of the world. Was that any reason for Him to make the Earth round?

"I don't care about money. I want a sensitive man. I want a man who will cry when I hit him."
-*Wendy Liebman*

"The male is a domestic animal which, if treated with firmness, can be trained to do most things."
-*Jilly Cooper*

He Said: Honey, I was in a terrible car accident. Sarah took me to the hospital. X-rays showed I broke both my legs and I might lose my right arm!

She Said: Who's Sarah?

"Man invented language to satisfy his deep need to complain." *-Lily Tomlin*

"I don't believe man is woman's natural enemy. Perhaps his lawyer is." *-Shana Alexander*

An English professor wrote the words, "Woman without her man is nothing" on the blackboard and asked his students to punctuate it.
The men wrote: "Woman, without her man, is nothing."
The women wrote: "Woman! Without her, man is nothing."

How can you be serious dating a man with a handlebar mustache?

He Said: What's for dinner tonight?

She Said: You've got two choices.

He Said: What are they?

She Said: Take it or leave it.

She Said: What?

He Said: I said...

She Said: (interrupting) It's not that I didn't hear you. I'm giving you a chance to change what you said.

"My, that's a beautiful diamond you have there," said one woman to the other.
"Yes, but it comes with a curse. This is the Klopman Diamond."
"Oh my!" said the wide-eyed admirer. "What's the curse?"
"Klopman."

A couple are playing golf and are on the ninth green when suddenly the husband collapses from a heart attack. "Help me," he groans to his wife.
The wife calls 911 on her cell phone, talks for a few minutes, picks up her putter, and lines up her putt.
Her husband raises his head off the green and stares at her. "I'm dying over here and you're putting?!"
"Don't worry, dear," says the wife calmly. "They found a doctor on the second hole and he's coming to help you."
"Well, how long will it take for him to get here?" he asks feebly.
"No time at all," says his wife. "Everybody's already agreed to let him play through."

"Men, your lives are less stressful. For one thing, what you are wearing now will be in style for the rest of your lives." *-Carol Siskind*

He Said: Go on. Don't be shy. Ask me out.

She Said: Okay. Go out.

"The only thing that keeps me from being happily married…is my husband." *-Andra Douglas*

"We had a lot in common. I loved him and he loved him." *-Shelley Winters*

"The last guy I went out with, he was just so - I don't know - hopeless. He said if I broke up with him that he would kill himself. And I broke up with him, but he's not dead yet. I want to call him up and be like, 'You know, what's the deal? I thought we had an agreement.'" *-Margaret Cho*

Three guys are on their lunch break, talking about their wives. Two of them are bragging about how they're the "man of the house" while the third remains silent. After a while, one of the guys says to the third fellow, "You've been pretty quiet, pal. What's the matter, does your wife boss you around?"

The third guy says, "Let me tell you guys something. Just the other night, my wife came to me crawling on her hands and knees."

The first two guys look at him astonishingly and one says, "What was the reason for that?"

"She said, 'Get out from under that bed and fight like a man you little weasel.'"

He Said: I saw you with another man at lunch today. I want an explanation and I want the truth!

She Said: Make up your mind. Which do you want?

Q: Why didn't the husband change the baby for two weeks?
A: Because on the diapers package it said, "15-30 lbs."

Q: What's the definition of cannibalism?
A: Men eating pork

Q: What do men and mascara have in common?
A: They both run at the first sign of emotion.

Q: What's the difference between a smart man and a stupid man?
A: Nothing - They both think they know everything.

Q: What's the difference between a singles bar and the circus?
A: At a circus, the clowns don't talk.

Q: How does a man plan for his future?
A: He buys two cases of beer instead of one.

"Men and women are different. I don't think men grow a brain until 26 or even 30. Girls mature a lot quicker." -*Cyndi Lauper*

He Said: I don't understand what you're talking about.

She Said: I don't have either the time or the crayons to explain it to you.

A man and a woman were at a fancy restaurant. They had placed their orders, but as the waitress was returning to bring their drinks, she noticed the man's head disappear under the tablecloth.
"Pardon me, ma'am, but I think your husband just slid under the table."
The woman calmly looked up at her and replied firmly, "No, my date just slid under the table. My husband just walked in the door."

Prosecutor: Why did you shoot your husband with a bow and arrow?
Defendant: I didn't want to wake the children.

He Said: I wear the pants in this relationship.

She Said: Fine, but they're capris.

"Ninety percent of men give the other ten percent a bad name." *-Alix Perrault*

"My husband always felt that a marriage and career don't mix. That's why he's never worked."
-Phyllis Diller

He Said: How did the car wind up in the kitchen?

She Said: I made a left at the living room.

A crowd of husbands is about to enter through the Pearly Gates when St. Peter roars, "Hold it right there! I want all of you who were henpecked husbands while on Earth to form a line to my right. The rest of you stand to my left."

All but one husband stands on the henpecked line. St. Peter turns to the guy standing alone and says, "How about you? What's your story?"

He replies sheepishly, "My wife told me to stand here."

Two cannibal women are talking. One says, "I don't know what to make of my husband."

The other one says, "Get a recipe book."

An aging Romeo approached an attractive girl in a bar and asked, "So where have you been all my life?"

She looked him over and said, "Well, for the first half of it, I wasn't even born."

"Women are cursed, and men are the proof."
-*Roseanne Barr*

He Said: I'd go to the end of the world for you!

She Said: Yeah, but would you stay there?

She Said: I just bought a ticket for the $50 million lottery.

He Said: Oh, yeah? Let me know when you win.

She Said: I'll leave you a note.

"I prefer balding men. Why would you want to run your hands through a man's hair when you could shove your fist right into his skull?"
-*Stephanie Hodge*

"Have you ever tried to imagine what the world would be like without men? I mean without smiling."
-*Maxine*

This guy in a bar notices a woman who comes to the tavern often and is always alone. He decides to make his move but she turns him down politely. "No thank you. I'm keeping myself pure until I meet the man of my dreams," she says.
The guy replies, "That must be tough."
"Oh, it doesn't bother me too much," she says, "but my husband isn't too thrilled about it."

A woman called the town paper to place an obituary notice for her husband. She wanted it to read, "Mulligan died."
The sales clerk said, "Would that be all? You could add three more words for the same price, lady."
The woman added, "Cadillac for sale."

He Said: How come no matter how much we fight, you stay calm, cool and collected?

She Said: Simple. Whenever we argue, I take out all my hostilities by cleaning the bathroom.

He Said: What? How does that help?

She Said: I use your toothbrush.

Adam stayed out late a few nights in a row and Eve became suspicious.
"You're running around with another woman!" she accused.
"What? There's no other woman!" Adam exclaimed. "You're it!"
That night, Adam was sleeping soundly when he was suddenly awakened by Eve poking him in the chest.
"What are you doing?"
"Counting your ribs."

A guy spoke to a genie and asked her to turn him into an irresistible and desirable hunk to all women. The genie turned him into a credit card.

Husband: I can't believe you just backed the car over my bike!
Wife: That's what you get for leaving it on the lawn.

"Husbands and boyfriends are the best people to share secrets with… They'll never tell anyone, because they aren't even listening." *-Jen Tomlinson*

He Said: I know how to please a woman.

She Said: Then why don't you please leave me alone.

A male and female executive were mistakenly assigned to the same sleeper on a train on their way to a convention. After much embarrassment, they decided to accept the situation and get some sleep. In the middle of the night, the man leaned down from his upper birth and tapped the woman.
"I'm awfully sorry to bother you, but I'm very cold. Could you hand me that blanket over there?"
"I have a better idea," the woman replied. "How about, just for tonight, we pretend we're married?"
"Great!" said the man, brightening.
"Good," said the woman. "Now get your own blanket!"

She Said: Why don't you ever wear your ring?

He Said: It cuts off my circulation.

She Said: I know. It's supposed to.

"As you get older, the pickings get slimmer, but the people don't." -*Carrie Fisher*

"This is my second marriage and I've learned, grown. If we have a fight, before we go to bed I always say three little words: 'I love you.' If that doesn't work, I say two little words: 'community property.'" -*JoAnne Astrow*

He Said: Are you a parking ticket? Because you've got FINE written all over you.

She Said: I like your approach. Now let's see your departure.

After the couple has another one of their many heated arguments, the wife calls her mother and says, "That did it. I'm tired of all these fights. I'm coming to live with you, Mom."
The mother replies, "No, dear. He needs to pay for his mistakes. I'm coming to live with you."

Walking along the beach, a woman finds a bottle. She rubs it and a genie appears.
"I'm your good news/bad news genie," the genie says.
"What does that mean?" the woman asks.
"The good news is that I'll grant you three wishes. The bad news is that for every wish you make, your ex-boyfriend will get the same thing, only double."
After thinking for a moment, the woman says, "For my first wish, I would like five million dollars."
"Okay, and your ex-boyfriend will get ten million dollars," the genie reminds her. "What else do you want?"
"I'd love to have a blue Porsche," the woman says. Instantly, the car appears on the beach and the genie says, "Now your ex has two Porsches. What is your third and final wish?"
The woman replies, "I would like to donate a kidney."

"Macho does not prove mucho." *-Zsa Zsa Gabor*

She Said: Honey, I have some good news and bad news about the car.

He Said: Gimme the good news first.

She Said: The air bag works.

"You know your date is old when you find out that his recreational vehicle is a Lazy Boy recliner."
-Joan Rivers

"Remarrying a man you've divorced is like having your appendix put back in." *-Phyllis Diller*

"When women are depressed, they either eat or go shopping. Men invade another country."
-Elayne Boosler

"A good place to meet a man is at the dry cleaners. These men usually have jobs and bathe."
-Rita Rudner

A guy wakes up from surgery and the doctor says,
"I've got good news and bad news."
The patient says, "Gimme the bad news first."
The doctor says, "Okay- during your operation, your girlfriend left you a message saying that she's leaving you for another man."
"Geez," says the guy. "What's the good news?"
The doctor says, "I'm picking her up at eight."

He Said: You've put on a few, haven't you?

She Said: Perhaps... but you should know about a recent study which found that women carrying a little extra weight live longer than the men who mention it.

Two old ladies met in the street. After inquiring about each other's health, the topic of conversation turned to their respective husbands.
Agnes: I was so sorry to hear about your husband. What happened?
Mabel: Oh, as you know, George raised vegetables. He went out to the garden to get some carrots one day last week and had a sudden, fatal heart attack.
Agnes: Oh, my. That's terrible. What did you do?
Mabel: I opened a can of string beans instead.

"It's not easy being a mother. If it were easy, fathers would do it." -*Dorothy,* The Golden Girls

"I met this guy who said he loved children, then I found out he was on parole for it." -*Monica Piper*

He Said: You could stand to lose a few, dear.

She Said: Would you like to see me back to my original weight?

He Said: That would be nice.

She Said: Seven and a half pounds isn't very realistic.

He Said: Can I buy you a drink?

She Said: Actually, I'd rather have the money.

An efficiency expert concluded his seminar with a cautionary note, saying, "Don't try these techniques at home without total preparation. Make sure you think through all of the possible scenarios."
An audience member piped up, "Why not?"
The expert explained, "Well, I made a lengthy study of my wife's breakfast routine. She made a number of trips between the refrigerator, the stove, the pantry and the table. For the most part, she carried just a single item at a time. Finally, after two years, I said to her, 'Dear, why don't you carry several items at once to save yourself some time?'"
"Did it save time?" the audience member asked.
"Yes, it did," answered the expert. "It used to take her 19 minutes to make breakfast. Now I do it in seven."

Of course, you've heard of the new "Divorce Barbie." It comes with all of Ken's stuff.

"Trust your husband, adore your husband, and get as much as you can in your own name."
-*Joan Rivers*

"I broke up with my boyfriend of five years. We would have broken up after the first two weeks, but new restaurants kept opening." -*Jann Karam*

He Said: You wear too much makeup.

She Said: You consume too much oxygen.

"The only problem with women is men."
-Kathie Sarachild

A woman welcomes her husband home, saying,
"Hi, Superman. Where have you been?"
"Working, as usual," says the hubby.
"How come you smell so nice, Superman?" she
continues.
"We had a meeting. When I dropped a pen, my
secretary bent over to pick it up at the same time
and we bumped into each other. You probably smell
her perfume."
"What about the lipstick on your collar, Superman?"
"I guess, as we bent over, her lips must have
accidentally brushed my collar."
"And what about the loose button, Superman?"
"Oh, that. The shirt got caught on the corner of the
table when I picked up the pen. The button must've
come undone. Say, why do you keep calling me
Superman?"
"Because only Superman wears his underwear over
his pants."

He Said: Knock-knock.

She Said: Who's there?

He Said: The love of your life.

She Said: Liar- you know chocolate can't talk.

He Said: You're a bit too thin for me.

She Said: That's okay. You're a bit too thick for me.

An elderly man was at home on his deathbed. He smelled the aroma of his favorite cookies baking. He craved for one last chocolate chip cookie before he died.

He fell out of bed, crawled to the landing, then down the stairs and finally to the kitchen where his wife was baking. With waning strength he made his way to the table and was just barely able to lift his arm to the cookie sheet. As he grasped a warm, moist cookie, his wife suddenly whacked his hand with a spatula.

"Why?" he meekly and weakly said, "did you do that?"

She replied, "Because they're for the funeral."

Guy: Will you marry me?
Girl: No.
And she lived happily ever after.

He Said: Can't you ever apologize?

She Said: Sure I can. I'm sorry I ever laid eyes on you.

"I'd marry again if I found a man who had $15 million and would sign over half of it to me before the marriage and guarantee that he'd be dead within a year." -*Bette Davis*

He Said: Just calm down.

She Said: Don't you tell me to calm down. You might as well stab me and ask why I'm bleeding.

Q: What makes a man think about a dinner by candlelight?
A: A power failure

Q: Why do jocks play on artificial turf?
A: To keep them from grazing

Q: What do you call a guy with an opinion?
A: Wrong

Q: Why are most dumb blonde jokes one-liners?
A: So men can understand them.

Q: How come men don't have a mid-life crisis?
A: They're stuck in adolescence.

Q: What do men and beer have in common?
A: They're both empty from the neck up.

Q: What has eight hands and an IQ of 160?
A: Four guys watching a football game.

"There are two perfectly good men, one dead and the other unborn." -*Chinese Proverb*

He Said: So how come you broke up with your ex?

She Said: Because my knight in shining armor turned out to be a loser in tin foil.

Bertha asked her husband for the newspaper. He replied, "Newspaper? My dear, we're living in a digital world and you're still asking for the newspaper? Here, take my iPad instead."
So she took the iPad and killed the cockroach.

"My first marriage was an appetizer marriage. A little guacamole marriage. I married a dip."
-JoAnne Astrow

"I have a hard time believing the story about the three wise men. One, maybe… but three?" -Maxine

"If women were in charge, all men's underwear would come with an expiration date." -Diane Ford

"Women get the last word in every argument. Anything a man says after that is the beginning of a new argument." -Tracy O'Mahony

"Men should be like Kleenex- soft, strong and disposable." -Cher

She Said: I can't believe it. You're shirtless and covered in oil!?

He Said: Well, you said I never glisten.

She Said: Listen! You never listen!!

"I joined a Nautilus club to meet men, but these guys are all bulk and no brains, like human sequoia trees. This one guy was so stupid he couldn't walk while I was chewing gum. I blew a bubble, and he stubbed his toe." -*Cathy Ladman*

Oscar had a blind date but, beforehand, he was worried what to do if she was really unattractive. His buddy told him, "No problem- there's an app for just that situation. It's called 'Mom Are You Ok?' and it schedules your phone to ring just after you meet your date. If you like her, you just ignore your phone. If you want to cut short the date, you answer with, 'Mom? What's the matter? Are you okay?' It works like a charm."

That evening, Oscar knocked on the girl's door and it turned out he needn't have worried at all. She was absolutely stunning! Just as he was about to say hello, her phone rang.

She answered it and said, "Mom? What's the matter? Are you okay?"

He Said: I liked your hair better when it was longer.

She Said: And I liked it better when you weren't talking.

He Said: C'mon, I wasn't that drunk last night.

She Said: Oh no, not at all. When we were in Walmart and the intercom came on, you dropped to your knees and screamed, "The LORD has spoken!"

Did you hear the one about the three dumb guys who went ice fishing but didn't catch anything? By the time they cut a hole big enough for the boat to fit in, it was time to go home.

Marriage is a relationship in which one person is always right, and the other is a husband.

As her husband was about to leave to go hunting, his wife said, "If wild game meat is too expensive, you can buy fish instead."

"Men are like fine wine. They all start out like grapes, and it's our job to stomp them and keep them in the dark until they mature into something you'd like to have dinner with." *-Kathleen Mifsud*

"I'm not good at being alone. Especially at the end of a day when my finances are a mess, my car is falling apart, I can't find my shoe. That's when I need a big strong guy to hold me close so I can look into his eyes, and blame him." *-Simone Alexander*

He Said: You're one in a million!

She Said: Yeah- and so are your chances.

"My husband thinks that health food is anything he eats before the expiration date." *-Rita Rudner*

"I had this boyfriend who told me he thought I needed to lose weight. He really hurt my feelings, but he was right. I'm proud to say I lost 173 pounds - when I dumped him. I can't tell you how much better I feel." *-Wendy Kamenoff*

A man and a woman were driving on the same road from opposite directions. As they passed, the woman leaned out of the car window and shouted, "Pig!" The man yelled back, "Witch!" Each continued on their way until the man rounded the next corner and crashed into a hog.

Guy: I hate all this modern art stuff. Look at that. It's garbage.
Girl: No, that's a Picasso.
Guy: What about this one with all these crazy colors and designs?
Girl: That's by Matisse.
Guy: How about this ridiculous piece of garbage where the guy's got a lopsided nose, a pencil neck, and bulging eyes?
Girl: That's a mirror.

She Said: You only know four vowels, don't you?

He Said: What do you mean by that?

She Said: You act as if you didn't know that I even existed.

Myrtle was telling her friend, Ethel, about her deceased husband.

"Just before he died, Fred told me that he had three envelopes in his top desk drawer that would take care of all the arrangements. So, when he died I opened the drawer and, sure enough, there were three envelopes. On the first envelope, Fred wrote 'For the Coffin.' There was four thousand dollars in the envelope, so I bought him a beautiful coffin. The next envelope was marked 'For Expenses.' With the five thousand dollars in that envelope, I was able to pay all funeral costs. The third envelope had six thousand dollars in it. Fred wrote 'For the Stone' on that envelope."

Myrtle held out her hand to Ethel and said, "Isn't it beautiful?"

He Said: Why won't you marry me? Is there someone else?

She Said: There must be.

"If you want a guy to do something for you, all you have to do is introduce an element of senseless danger, and it becomes a sport. 'Honey, why don't you try to take out the trash - while I chase you on rollerblades with a chainsaw!'" *-C. Lynn Mitchell*

She Said: What do you do?

He Said: I'm an IT.

She Said: What is that? Something that's missing the "DIO" in the middle?

"They say marriage is a contract. No, it's not. Contracts come with warrantees. When something goes wrong, you can take it back to the manufacturer. If your husband starts acting up, you can't take him back to his mama's house. 'I don't know; he just stopped working. He's just laying around making a funny noise.'" -*Wanda Sykes*

A husband and wife were not on speaking terms. Before turning in for the night, the husband remembered he needed his wife, always an early riser, to wake him up at 5 a.m. so he could catch an early business flight. Stubborn about breaking the silence between them, he left a note on her pillow that read, "Please wake me up at 5 a.m."
The next morning he woke up at eight and missed his flight. He was fuming that his wife had not awakened him, only to find a note on his bedside table- "It's 5 o'clock. Wake up."

She Said: Can you make a noise like a frog?

He Said: Sure, babe, but why would you want me to do that?

She Said: Because when you croak, I'm taking the kids to Disney World.

He Said: You're late again!

She Said: It's better to arrive late than arrive ugly.

"My boyfriend and I broke up because I went over to his house unannounced. He was upset that I'd come over without calling first, especially since he was there with another woman. He trusted me, and I let him down." *-Grace White*

This fellow walks by an optometrist's shop. Displayed in the storefront window is a gigantic pair of sunglasses accompanied by a sign, "Nudie Sunglasses!" The chap is intrigued, goes inside and asks the optometrist about them. The optometrist says, "Try them on and see for yourself."
The guy tries on the giant sunglasses, looks at the optometrist and can't believe what he sees. The optometrist appears totally naked! "Does this mean that when I put on these sunglasses everyone becomes nude?"
"That's right."
Well, the guy just has to have them, so he buys a pair and heads home. When he gets there, he opens the door, puts on his new nudie sunglasses and walks into the living room. There he sees his wife sitting on the couch with his neighbor, both appearing to be stark naked. "You're not going to believe this, dear," says the guy, "but I just bought these super duper sunglasses."
He takes them off to show her and notices the wife and neighbor are still nude.
"Geez," he complains, "I've only had these sunglasses half an hour and they're broken already!"

He Said: You should stop lifting weights or you're gonna look like a man.

She Said: Maybe you should start so you will.

"The trouble with some women is that they get all excited about nothing - and then marry him." *-Cher*

"Give your relationship attention like you would a plant. You have to water it every day and give it sunshine. So put your man out in the sun and spray him with a hose." *-Whitney Cummings*

"Women speak because they wish to speak, whereas a man speaks only when driven to speech by something outside himself - like, for instance, he can't find any clean socks." *-Jean Kerr*

A man and his wife enter a dentist's office.
The wife says, "I need to have a tooth pulled. No gas or Novacaine -- I'm in a hurry. Just pull the tooth as quickly as possible."
"You're a brave woman," remarks the dentist. "Now, show me which one it is."
The wife turns to her husband and says, "Open your mouth and show the dentist which tooth it is, dear."

He Said: Can I have your number?

She Said: Get your own number.

She Said: Okay, you say you're so smart. Spell Mississippi.

He Said: The river or the state?

Q: What do men and diapers have in common?
A: Both have to be changed regularly and for the same reason.

Q: What's the definition of a lazy man?
A: One who gets someone to read the DIY manual to him

Q: How come men only get half-hour lunch breaks?
A: So their bosses won't need to retrain them

Q: Why do men like BMWs?
A: Because they can spell it.

Q: What do you call a man with half a brain?
A: Gifted

Q: How many men does it take to wallpaper a room?
A: It depends how thinly you slice them.

"When you're first single, you're so optimistic. At the beginning, you're like, 'I want to meet a guy who's really smart, really sweet, really good-looking, has a really great career.' Six months later, you're like, 'Lord, any mammal with a day job.'" -*Carol Leifer*

He Said: Shall we see a movie?

She Said: I've already seen it.

"I never married because there was no need. I have three pets at home which answer the same purpose as a husband. I have a dog which growls every morning, a parrot which swears all afternoon and a cat that comes home late at night." *-Marie Corelli*

A guy was shopping for dinner at a supermarket when a beautiful redhead smiled and waved at him. He couldn't figure out where he knew her from but nonetheless he was thrilled at the attention until she walked up and said, "I think you're the father of one of my kids."

Taken aback, he initially denied it but then searched his memory. "Wait," he blurted out. "That night my buddies got me drunk and took all my clothes and set me out on Main Street and I wandered around until I came into this little bar and fell in the mud-wrestling pit and vomited all over the floor... Were you the stripper who took me home with her that night?"

"No," she answered coolly. "I'm your son's math teacher."

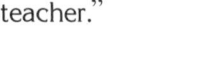

Polly: I had a double-whammy of a bad day.
Molly: What happened?
Polly: My ex got run over by a bus.
Molly: Wow! What else happened?
Polly: I got fired from my bus driving job.

He Said: You're never on time.

She Said: What do you mean? This is the earliest I've ever been late.

"I still miss my ex-husband. (But my aim is improving.)" -*Tracy Nichols*

"As long as you know men are like children you know everything." -*Coco Chanel*

"Give a man a fish and he has food for a day; teach him how to fish and you can get rid of him for the entire weekend." -*Zenna Schaffer*

"I love being married. It's so great to find that one special person to annoy for the rest of your life." -*Rita Rudner*

All together now, "If you're happy and you know it, thank your ex…"

A daughter asked her mother, "What are qualities that I should look for in a spouse? You know, for someone that I will be spending eternity with."
The mother answered, "Go ask your father. He did better than I did."

He Said: Will you marry me?

She Said: I'm thinking about it.

He Said: What is there to think about?

She Said: I'm thinking if you're the man I want my children to spend every other weekend with.

Herb calls his wife from work and says, "Honey, the boss surprised us with a weekend fishing trip. We're leaving in just a few hours. I'm in a hurry. Please pack my bags and I'll pick 'em up in a few."
He goes home, picks up his bags and his fishing gear and rushes off.
When he returns home his wife asks, "Did you have a good trip, dear?"
Herb replies, "Yes, but you forgot to pack some underwear."
The wife says, "Oh no, I didn't. They were in the tackle box."

One day a guy asked a genie to make him smarter than any other man on earth. The genie turned him into a woman.

"A man in love is like a clipped coupon - it's time to cash in." *-Mae West*

He Said: Haven't I seen you someplace before?

She Said: Yes, that's why I don't go there anymore.

He Said: You look like a dream.

She Said: Go back to sleep.

"Men, if you've ever been given a fake phone number, it means you scare women. Basically, it says, 'I'd reject you to your face, but I'm afraid that my head would wind up in the garbage and my body in the bay. So here's a phony number. Hopefully, you won't figure that out until I've made my escape.'"
-Lori Chapman

"A man will go to war, fight and die for his country. But he won't get a bikini wax." *-Rita Rudner*

How are men like blenders?
You need one, but you're not quite sure why.

What does the smart guy do at the M&M factory?
Proof-read

What do you call a handcuffed man?
Trustworthy

He Said: Am I the first man you ever kissed?

She Said: Maybe. Were you at the 2012 Mardi Gras?

He Said: I don't understand how you can be so beautiful and so stupid at the same time.

She Said: Allow me to explain. God made me beautiful so you'd be attracted to me; God made me stupid so I'd be attracted to you.

The hunting season's just begun- opening day -and Herb's all prepared. The SUV's loaded up, he's anxiously on his way out the door and suddenly the phone rings. Herb yells to his wife, "If someone asks for me, I'm already gone."
The wife answers, "Yes, he's still here."
"Geez," Herb complains, "I told you to say I left already."
"Yeah, I know, but it wasn't you they asked for."

Priest: My deepest sympathy, Bertha. I'm so sorry to hear of Clyde's passing.
Widow: Thank you, Father.
Priest: I know it's a difficult time. I just want you to know that I'll be here for you.
Widow: I appreciate that, Father.
Priest: Tell me, Bertha. Did Clyde have any last requests?
Widow: Yes he did, Father.
Priest: What was that, may I ask?
Widow: He asked me to please put the gun down.

"My ex-boyfriend's mother told me she felt my material was men-bashing, and that I hate men. I said, 'I don't hate all men, just your son. That's just one guy.'" -*Laura Kightlinger*

She Said: You're illiterate!

He Said: The joke's on you. My parents were married.

A guy was on a plane trip and was assigned a seat next to a gorgeous young woman.
As he sat down next to her he coyly asked, "Does the airline charge you extra for sitting next to good-looking men?"
She replied, "Yes, but I wasn't prepared to pay."

"How you doin'?" the doctor asked Cliff.
"Terrific," he replied. "I've found religion. I've got poor eyesight and God knew that so He fixed things for me. Now when I get up in the middle of the night to use the bathroom- like magic -the light goes on, and then- poof! -it goes off when I'm done."
The doctor was concerned about this so he called Cliff's wife later in the day and said, "Cliff told me he found God and that when he gets up during the night to use the bathroom, the light magically turns on and then off when he's through. Is this true?"
"No, said Cliff's wife. "It means he's been peeing in the refrigerator again."

"A man in love is incomplete until he is married. Then he's finished." *-Zsa Zsa Gabor*

He Said: I can't live without you.

She Said: Lighten up. I won't quit my job.

He Said: I like a girl with no makeup.

She Said: Yeah, well I like a guy with no opinions, so I guess we're both disappointed.

A widower rarely got along his wife. Nonetheless, he found himself missing her tremendously. Desperate to contact her, he went to see a psychic. The psychic went into a trance. A slight breeze rippled through the dimly lit room, and suddenly the man heard his late wife's voice.

"Dear!" he cried. "Is that you?"

"Yes it is."

"Are you happy?"

"Yes, more than you could ever imagine."

"Happier than you were with me?"

"Yes, I am."

"Then Heaven must be an amazing place!"

"I'm not in Heaven, dear."

He Said: You may think you're miss smarty pants because you've got a degree, but I've got street smarts.

She Said: Sure you're street smart. Sesame Street smart.

"Women love men in a patronizing way, kind of how you love the village idiot." *-Susie Essman*

"Honesty is the key to a relationship. If you can fake that, you're in." *-Courteney Cox*

He Said: I like the way you die the roots of your hair brown.

She Said: Yeah, well at least I've got some roots.

"Whatever women do they must do twice as well as men to be thought half as good. Luckily, this is not difficult." -*Charlotte Witton*

"Guys are lucky because they get to grow mustaches. I wish I could. It's like having a little pet for your face." -*Anita Wise*

"What's with you men? Would hair stop growing on your chest if you asked directions somewhere?" -*Erma Bombeck*

I know a guy who's really dumb. He said onions are the only food that makes you cry. So I threw a coconut at his face.

The winner of the worldwide Perfect Man contest has been named. He's MR. POTATO HEAD!

- He's tan.
- He's cute.
- He knows how to accessorize.
- And if he looks at another girl, you can rearrange his face.

He Said: I'm dating your ex.

She Said: Cool, I'm eating a sandwich… want those leftovers, too?

On their 40th wedding anniversary, a fairy appeared at the home of a 65-year-old married couple and said to the husband, "Your wife told me that you've been the perfect husband since the day you were married. I would like to fulfill a wish, any wish, of yours in honor of your anniversary."
"Very well," responded the husband as he turned to his wife and said, "I am so sorry dear, but I'll never get another wish like this again." He turned to the fairy and said, "I would like to spend my remaining years with a woman 25 years younger than me."
The fairy smiled, winked at the woman and said, "I figured as much."
With that, she waved her magic wand and -poof!- the man became 90 years old.

"Going out with a jerky guy is kind of like having a piece of food caught in your teeth. All your friends notice it before you do." *-Livia Squires*

"I'm not upset I'm divorced. I'm only upset I'm not a widow." *-Roseanne Barr*

"My husband and I had a very messy divorce because there was a baby involved. Him. And I didn't want custody." *-Wendy Liebman*

He Said: Men like me don't just grow on trees ya know.

She Said: I know. They swing from them.

Q: What's the difference between your ex and a trampoline?
A: You take off your shoes to jump on a trampoline.

Q: How many men does it take to screw in a light bulb?
A: One... He just holds the bulb up and waits for the room to revolve around him.

Q: What do you call a man who's lost 80% of his intelligence?
A: Divorced

Q: How do you get a man to do sit-ups?
A: Put the remote control between his toes.

Q: What do you call an intelligent, good looking, sensitive man?
A: A rumor

"Men and women have always had problems relating. As children, men were told: 'Be a man. Don't cry!' and women were told, 'Let it out. Cry. You'll feel better!' And that's why as adults, women become very emotional, and men become snipers."
-*Pam Stone*

He Said: If you kiss me, I promise I won't turn into a frog.

She Said: So why would I want to kiss you?

One afternoon, a man was reading the newspaper when his wife suddenly snuck up behind him and hit him on the head with a frying pan. "What did you do that for?!" he shouted.

"I found a piece of paper in your jacket pocket with the name 'Caroline' on it," she answered.

"Geez, babe, when I went to the track last week with my buddies, that was the name of the horse I was betting on."

His wife became silent, but four days later he was reading the newspaper again when she hit him one more time on the head with the pan. "Now what did you hit me for?!?" he snapped.

She said, "Your horse called."

"You may marry the man of your dreams, but 14 years later, you're married to a couch that burps."
-Roseanne Barr

"Before marriage, a man declares that he would lay down his life to serve you; after marriage, he won't even lay down his newspaper to talk to you."
-Helen Rowland

He Said: I loved you terribly.

She Said: Yes, you did.

He Said: Why don't we go back to my place for some heavy breathing?

She Said: Why? Is your elevator out of order?

"Men are like bank accounts. Without a lot of money they don't generate a lot of interest." *-Sandi Sola*

"Men are like pumpkins. It seems like all the good ones are either taken or they've had everything scraped out of their heads with a spoon."
-Lori Bealler

A man and his wife were out for a drive when a cop pulled them over. As the officer approached the car, the man rolled down his window.

The cop said, "Excuse me, sir. Were you aware that you were driving well over the speed limit?"

The driver responded, "Why, no officer, I wasn't aware of that."

With that, his wife exclaimed, "Who are you kidding? You were going at least 20 miles over the limit!"

The cop then asked, "And I noticed you weren't wearing a seat belt. How come?"

He answered, "Well, officer, when I saw you approach the car I figured I'd probably have to get out so I took it off."

His wife then said, "What are you talking about? You never wear a seat belt."

At that point, the cop leaned in and said to the wife, "Does your husband always lie like this?"

"Oh, not always Officer," she replied. "Only when he's had too much to drink."

He Said: What's it like being the best-looking person in the room?

She Said: You'll never know.

A guy walks into a bar with a pig under his arm. The bartender says, "Where did you get that?"
The pig says, "I won him in a raffle."

A cop calls the police station and says, "I've got a crime to report. A woman shot her husband for stepping on the floor she just mopped."
The sergeant at the police desk asks, "Did you arrest her?"
"No, not yet. The floor is still wet."

He Said: You're the reason they have to put directions on shampoo.

She Said: I'm sorry, but in order for you to insult me, I first have to value your opinion. Nice try, though.

"Never trust a husband too far or a bachelor too near." *-Helen Rowland*

"I went out with a guy once who told me I didn't need to drink to make myself more fun to be around. I told him, 'I'm drinking so that you're more fun to be around.'" *-Chelsea Handler*

She Said: You've been drinking, haven't you?

He Said: No.

She Said: Make up your mind. It's me or the bar.

He Said: It's you. I can tell by the voice.

This fellow proposed to a beautiful woman, pointing out that he was an eligible bachelor of the highest sort, primarily because his filthy rich father was 98 years old and that he was the heir to his dad's fortune.
The woman said she needed some time to think about his offer. Three weeks later, she became his step-mother.

"Men who consistently leave the toilet seat up secretly want women to get up to go the bathroom in the middle of the night and fall in." *-Rita Rudner*

"I love it when my husband thinks I might leave him. He gets so insecure, he does the dishes. But I'd have to file for divorce papers to get him to clean the toilet." *-Shirley Lipner*

She Said: It's about time you did something around here. Why don't you go water the plants?

He Said: But it's raining.

She Said: Take an umbrella.

He Said: If I could see you naked, I'd die happy.

She Said: If I saw you naked, I'd probably die laughing.

Farnsworth and his wife, Edith, were having breakfast one morning when the Mrs. said, "You probably don't know what day this is, do you?"
"Of course I do," Farnsworth huffily replied as he got up to leave for work.
A couple of hours later, the doorbell rang. When Edith opened the door, she was presented with a dozen roses. Shortly after noon, there was another delivery. This time it was a box of her favorite chocolates. The doorbell rang again shortly after five, when an enormous fruit basket was delivered.
When Farnsworth came home, Edith excitedly said, "A dozen roses, a box of chocolates, and a beautiful fruit basket. This is the best Groundhog Day I've ever had!"

On the wall in a ladies room: "My husband follows me everywhere..."
Written just below it: "I do not!"

"I like the concept of 'men.' It's the reality I have trouble with." -*Stephanie H. Piro*

"The difference between government bonds and men is that government bonds mature."
-*Debbie Perry*

She Said: Have you ever read Shakespeare?

He Said: No, who wrote it?

"I'd like to make the world a better place, but how do you fly three and a half billion men to another planet?" *-Maxine*

"My husband said he needed more space. So I locked him outside." *-Roseanne Barr*

"The ideal man doesn't smoke, doesn't drink, doesn't do drugs, doesn't swear, doesn't get angry, doesn't exist." *-Robin Kreismer*

"Women want mediocre men, and men are working hard to become as mediocre as possible." *-Margaret Mead*

Did you hear about the divorce lawyer who did a mailing to all the married male members of the exclusive country club?
She sent out 175 Valentines signed "Guess who?"

He Said: You're too gorgeous to be single.

She Said: You're too ugly to be flirting with me.

He Said: I just put my laundry in the fridge. Sometimes I think I'm an idiot.

She Said: Oh, I do that all the time.

He Said: Put your laundry in the fridge?

She Said: No, think you're an idiot.

Three men were trapped on an island and needed to get across the water to the mainland. A bottle washed ashore. One of the men rubbed it and out popped a genie who said, "I will grant each of you one wish."
The first guy said, "Turn me into a fish," and he was able to swim across the water to the mainland.
The second guy said, "Give me a boat," and he rowed to the other side.
The third man said, "Turn me into a woman" and he was able to walk across the bridge.

"They say that the secret to a successful marriage is not to go to bed angry. So I was awake for two years." -*Wendy Liebman*

"Men are simple things. They can survive a whole weekend with only three things: beer, boxer shorts, and batteries for the remote control." -*Diana Jordan*

He Said: I'm reading up on Middle East politics.

She Said: I hope you realize the Gaza Strip isn't a topless bar.

He Said: I can see forever in your eyes.

She Said: All I see is never in yours.

"There is a vast difference between the savage and the civilized man, but it is never apparent to their wives until after breakfast." *-Helen Rowland*

"A woman without a man is like a fish without a bicycle." *-Gloria Steinem*

Geraldine called her insurance agent and told him that her house had burned down. "It was insured for $300,000, so I expect I'll be reimbursed for that amount."

"Wait just a sec," said the agent. "We'll determine how much your home is worth and then provide you with a comparable one."

"Oh, so that's how it works," said Geraldine. "In that case, I'd like you to cancel the policy on my husband."

Did you hear the one about the guy who returned a tie he got as a Christmas gift?
It was too tight.

And then there was the guy whose girlfriend told him she wanted to see more of the world. He bought her a globe.

He Said: You're one of my most trusted employees. I know you'll give me an honest answer to this simple question: Who's the stupid one, you or me?

She Said: Everyone knows you wouldn't hire stupid people.

Gertrude: How was your blind date?
Milly: Terrible. He showed up in his 1948 Rolls Royce.
Gertrude: What's so bad about that?
Milly: He's the original owner.

"The average woman would rather have beauty than brains, because the average man can see better than he can think." *-Vicky Perry*

"Why do men like intelligent women? Because opposites attract." *-Kathy Lette*

"There are easier things in life than trying to find a nice guy... like nailing a jellyfish to a tree for example." *-Pat Pereira*

He Said: A lot of women are going to be feeling mighty terrible when I get married.

She Said: Really? How many women are you planning to marry?

She Said: I love you.

He Said: Is that you or the wine talking?

She Said: It's me, talking to the wine.

Q: What do you call a woman who works as hard as a man?
A: Lazy

Q: Why are men like commercials?
A: You can't believe a word they say.

Q: How can you tell the difference between men's real gifts and their guilt gifts?
A: Guilt gifts are nicer.

Q: Why don't men make ice cubes?
A: They don't know the recipe.

Q: If a man and woman both jumped off a high building, why would the woman land first?
A: The man would get lost on the way.

Q: What's the quickest way of losing excess fat?
A: Divorce him.

"I'd much rather be a woman than a man. Women can cry, they can wear cute clothes, and they are the first to be rescued off of sinking ships."
-Gilda Radner

He Said: A thought just crossed my mind.

She Said: It must have been a long journey.

On a wild and windy day along a rocky Maine beach, a woman stumbled upon an ancient lamp. She picked it up, rubbed it, and a genie appeared.

"I am the genie of the lamp and... I'm sure you know how this goes lady. Just one disclaimer: due to downsizing and cutbacks, you only get one wish- not three- so make it a good one."

"Well, goodness, that isn't difficult. I wish for politicians in Washington to stop lying and cheating and fighting so they could start working on the problems of the country."

"A fair and efficient government?" the genie replied incredulously.

With that, the woman drew a rough chart in the sand with a stick.

"I especially want you to work on Congress. Here is the Senate and here is the House of Representatives. They are in gridlock and there's no compromise anymore. Nothing gets done. I want you to fix that."

The genie was shocked. "Listen lady, I'm good but not that good. You'll have to make another wish."

Thinking it over for a moment, the woman brightened and said, "Well I've never been able to find Mr. Right. I want a man who isn't obsessed with sports, who can express emotion, who is oblivious to other women and who doesn't mind cleaning."

The genie gave her a blank stare for a moment and then said, "Let me see that chart again."

"When a man brings his wife flowers for no reason, there's a reason." *-Molly McGee*

She Said: Can you imagine how hot I'd be if I exercised and ate right?

He Said: No doubt about it!

She Said: Well, I'm not gonna do it, but you can imagine.

A woman complained to her mother, "Men are only good for one thing."
"You got that right," her mom answered, "and how often do you have to double park?"

Sylvia: Aren't you wearing your wedding ring on the wrong finger?
Gladys: Yes, I am. I married the wrong man.

"Done with dating sites... I'm now focusing on pizza delivery guys because at least I know they have a job, a car, and pizza." -@*LINDAINDISGUISE*

"I married a younger man. Five years younger than I am. I figure it like this: If you can't find a good man, raise one." -*Wanda Sykes*

He Said: Hey, babe. Do you ever fantasize about me?

She Said: Why, yes- about you doing the dishes, mowing the lawn, vacuuming...

He Said: You're not too much of a looker, but I'd like to go out with you.

She Said: Thanks. You must be very open-minded. Is that how your brain slipped out?

"Whatever you may look like, marry a man your own age. As your looks begin to fade, so will his eyesight." *-Phyllis Diller*

"Marrying a man is like buying something you've been admiring for a long time in a shop window. You may love it when you get it home, but it doesn't always go with everything in the house." *-Jean Kerr*

He Said: I think it's about time I told you I'm having an affair.

She Said: Really? Who's the caterer?

A guy goes to a store and asks a saleswoman for some help to buy his girlfriend a birthday gift. The saleswoman shows him a $100 bracelet.
He says, "Way too much. What else have you got?"
She walks him over to the cosmetics counter, shows him a $25 bottle of perfume and says, "How about this?"
"Nah, still too expensive. Can you show me something really cheap?"
She handed him a mirror.

He Said: Before I die, sweetheart, I have to confess something to you.

She Said: I already know. That's why I poisoned you.

Watching the evening news, Harry was irked by an item that Stefi Vavoom, his favorite actress, had married a pro basketball player who was well-known for his sleazy and arrogant personality. "I'll never understand why the biggest jerks always get the most beautiful women!" Harry huffed.
His wife blushed and said, "Why thank you, Harry."

Two guys are out hunting when one of them looks down and says, "Look, deer tracks."
The other one says, "Nah, those are moose tracks. I know moose tracks when I see 'em."
A few seconds later, they both got run over by a train.

"I've heard that dogs are man's best friend. That explains where men are getting their hygiene tips."
-Kelly Maguire

"A good man doesn't just happen. They have to be created by us women. A guy is a lump like a doughnut. So, first you gotta get rid of all the stuff his mom did to him, and then you gotta get rid of all that macho crap that they pick up from beer commercials. And then there's my personal favorite, the male ego." *-Roseanne Barr*

He Said: You really hate me, don't you?

She Said: Not true. I just said that if you were on fire, I might consider roasting marshmallows. Big difference.

"What men don't realize is how many women date just so they won't have to cook dinner."
-Melanie White

"When you're wondering whether she's his daughter or his girlfriend, she's his girlfriend."
-Pamela Druckerman

Why did God create man before woman?
He needed a rough draft before the final copy.

How do you bring a sparkle to a man's eyes?
Shine a torch in his ear.

Why do men need instant replay on TV?
Because after 30 seconds they forget what happened.

How do you save a man from drowning?
Take your foot off his head.

What do men and women have in common?
They both distrust men.

He Said: You know, I think our kids got my brain.

She Said: I think so. I still have mine.

The patient's family gathered to hear what the surgeons had to say.

"Things don't look good. The only hope is a brain transplant. This is an experimental procedure. Now it might work, but the bad news is that brains are very expensive, and you will have to pay the cost yourselves."

"Well, how much does a brain cost?" asked one of the relatives.

"For a male brain, $500,000. For a female brain, $250,000."

Some of the male relatives tried to look surprised, but nodded in understanding, and a few actually smiled. Then the patient's daughter asked, "Why the big difference in price between male brains and female brains?"

"Oh, it's a standard pricing practice," said the head surgeon. "Women's brains are marked down because they've been used."

He Said: Is this seat empty?

She Said: Yep, and this one will be too if you sit down.

"If a man lies to you, don't get mad; get even. I once dated a guy who waited three months into our relationship before he told me he was married. I said, 'Hey, don't worry about it. I used to be a man.'"
-Livia Squires

He Said: How does it feel to be pleasingly plump?

She Said: I can lose the weight, but you'll always be ugly.

A woman inserted an advertisement in the classifieds: "Husband Wanted."
The next day she received more than 50 letters.
They all said the same thing: "You can have mine."

Molly: All Larry and I do is fight. I've been so upset that I've lost 15 pounds.
Jane: Gee, I'm sorry to hear that. You two should try to patch things up.
Molly: Not just yet. I've got another five pounds to go.

He Said: Where have you been all my life?

She Said: In your wildest dreams, where I'll be for the rest of your life.

"I was out on a date recently and the guy took me horseback riding. That was kind of fun, until we ran out of quarters." *-Susie Loucks*

"Most women set out to try to change a man, and when they have changed him they do not like him."
-Marlene Dietrich

She Said: Sweetie, if you'll make the toast and pour the coffee, breakfast will be ready.

He Said: Okay, great. What's for breakfast?

She Said: Toast and coffee.

"A man's got to do what a man's got to do. A woman must do what he can't." -*Rhonda Hansome*

"A divorcee is a women who got married so she didn't have to work, but now works so she doesn't have to get married." -*Anna Magnani*

"I'm still going on bad dates, when by now I should be in a bad marriage." -*Laura Kightlinger*

A young guy tells his mother that he's fallen in love and is going to get married.

He says, "Just for fun, Mom, I'm going to bring over three girls and you try to guess which woman I'm going to marry."

The mother agrees so the next day, the son brings three gorgeous women into the house. All three sit down on the living room couch and have a conversation with the guy's mother. After they leave, the son says, "OK, guess which one I'm going to marry."

The mother immediately answers, "The one in the middle."

"Incredible, Mom! You're right. How did you know?" His mother says, "I don't like her."

He Said: Mornin,' babe. Are you okay?

She Said: I guess…Why?

He Said: Because you spent the entire night cursing me in your sleep.

She Said: Who says I was asleep?

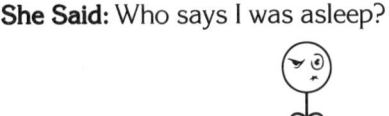

"When you are in love with someone you want to be near him all the time, except when you are out buying things and charging them to him."
-Miss Piggy

"If men can run the world, why can't they stop wearing neckties? How intelligent is it to start the day by tying a little noose around your neck?"
-Linda Ellerbee

Maybe you heard about the famous narcissist who was so full of himself that he figured the whole world revolved around him. One day he went to a nursing home, saw an elderly woman in the lobby and arrogantly said, "Hey lady, do you know who I am?" She responded, "No, but if you ask at the front desk they'll tell you."

At the breakfast table…

He Said: Every time I drink a cup of coffee I get this intense stinging in my eye.

She Said: Take the spoon out of the cup before you drink from it.

He Said: Honey, was I the first?

She Said: Why does everyone have to ask me that question?

Three men and a beautiful young girl are in the same compartment of a passenger train. They engage in conversation which soon becomes somewhat suggestive. At one point, the young girl says, "If each of you will give me $1, I will show you my legs."
The men all eagerly give her a buck. The girl pulls up her dress a bit to show her legs and then says, "If each of you fellows will give me $10, I'll show you my thighs."
The guys each give her a ten and the girl pulls up her dress to reveal even more of her legs. Then the young beauty says, "Now, for $100, I will show you where I was operated on for appendicitis."
All three give her the money. The girl then turns to the window and points outside at a building the train is passing. "See there, off in the distance. That's the hospital where I had it done!"

"Before marriage, a man will lie awake all night thinking about something you said; after marriage, he'll fall asleep before you finish saying it."
-Helen Rowland

He Said: At least we were the same age when we were married. Your new husband's 12 years younger than you. What are you, a cougar?

She Said: Why not? You were a cheetah.

He Said: You'll never find anyone like me.

She Said: That's the point.

"Behind every successful man is a surprised woman." *-Marion Pearson*

"The best way to get most husbands to do something is to suggest that perhaps they're too old to do it." *-Shirley MacLaine*

Q: What's the only time you can change a man?
A: When he's a baby

Q: How do you get a man to stop biting his nails?
A: Make him wear shoes.

Q: What should you give a man who has everything?
A: A woman to show him how to work it

Q: What do you do when your boyfriend walks out?
A: Shut the door.

Q: Why is the track at the Indy 500 oval?
A: So men won't have to stop and ask for directions.

Q: How did the girl break up with the tractor driver?
A: She sent him a John Deere letter.

She Said: I have some bad news and some worse news.

He Said: What's the bad news?

She Said: I ran over your golf clubs.

He Said: Geez! What's the worse news?

She Said: They were on the front porch.

An attractive secretary, often subjected to her boss's unwanted advances, goes to confession and says, "Forgive me Father, for I have sinned. I went skiing and saw my boss on the same slope. He didn't recognize me because I was wearing a ski mask. So, I skied over to where he was, gave him a push and roared with laughter as he rolled over and over down the hill, breaking his leg in three places."
"Why are you telling me this again?" asked the priest. That's the fifth time you've confessed this sin."
The secretary answers, "I know. I just like talking about it."

"I've always said we got married because there was nothing on TV." -*Bette Midler*

"Behind every successful man is a woman. Behind her is his wife." -*Linda Anderson*

"A man without a woman is a bachelor. A woman without a man is a genius." -*Maxine*

He Said: Wow, is it hot today! What will the neighbors think if I mow the lawn without my shirt on?

She Said: Probably that I married you for your money.

"The older theory was, marry an older man because they're more mature. But the new theory is men don't mature. Marry a younger one." *-Rita Rudner*

What is the difference between a man and childbirth?
One can be terribly painful and sometimes almost unbearable while the other is the incomparable joy of having a baby.

What is the one thing that men at singles bars have in common?
They're married.

What happened to the man who put odor-eaters in his shoes?
He disappeared.

How are men like paper cups?
They're both dispensable.

Why did Dorothy get lost in Oz?
She had three men giving her directions.

He Said: When I die, I want you to sell all of my things.

She Said: Why would you want me to do that?

He Said: Well, I figure you'll get married again and I don't want some other jerk using my stuff.

She Said: What makes you think I'd marry another jerk?

"Sometimes I wonder if men and women really suit each other. Perhaps they should live next door and just visit now and then." *-Katherine Hepburn*

"A man on a date wonders if he'll get lucky. A woman already knows." *-Monica Piper*

How do you know when a man is about to say something smart?
When he starts his sentence with, "A woman once told me...."

What's the best way to get a man to remember your anniversary?
Get married on his birthday.

He Said: I got a bottle of wine for my mother.

She Said: Nice trade.